Research in Criminology

Series Editors
Alfred Blumstein
David P. Farrington

Research in Criminology

Understanding and Controlling Crime: Toward A New Research Strategy
David P. Farrington, Lloyd E. Ohlin and James Q. Wilson

The Social Ecology of Crime
J.M. Byrne and R.J. Sampson (Eds.)

The Reasoning Criminal: Rational Choice Perspectives on Offending
Derek B. Cornish and Ronald V. Clarke (Eds.)

The Social Contexts of Criminal Sentencing
Martha A. Myers and Susette M. Talarico

Predicting Recidivism Using Survival Models
Peter Schmidt and Ann Dryden Witte

Coping, Behavior, and Adaptation in Prison Inmates
Edward Zamble and Frank J. Porporino

Prison Crowding: A Psychological Perspective
Paul B. Paulus

Off School, In Court: An Experimental and Psychiatric Investigation of Severe School Attendance Problems
I. Berg, I. Brown and R. Hullin

Policing and Punishing the Drinking Driver: A Study of General and Specific Deterrence
Ross Homel

Judicial Decision Making, Sentencing Policy, and Numerical Guidance
Austin Lovegrove

Criminal Behavior and the Justice System: Psychological Perspectives
Hermann Wegener, Friedrich Lösel and Jochen Haisch (Eds.)

Male Criminal Activity from Childhood Through Youth: Multilevel and Developmental Perspectives
Marc Le Blanc and Marcel Fréchette

continued after index

Anne L. Schneider

Deterrence and Juvenile Crime

Results from a National Policy Experiment

With 12 Illustrations

Springer-Verlag
New York Berlin Heidelberg
London Paris Tokyo Hong Kong

Anne L. Schneider
College of Public Programs, Arizona State University,
Tempe, Arizona 85287, USA

Senior Research Analyst
Laurie H. Ervin
Department of Political Science, Oklahoma State University,
Stillwater, Oklahoma 74074, USA

Series Editors
Alfred Blumstein
School of Urban and Public Affairs, Carnegie-Mellon University,
Pittsburgh, Pennsylvania 15213, USA

David P. Farrington
Institute of Criminology, University of Cambridge,
Cambridge CB3 9DT, England, UK

Library of Congress Cataloging-in-Publication Data
Schneider, Anne L.
Deterrence and juvenile crime : results from a national policy experiment / Anne L. Schneider.
p. cm. — (Research in criminology)
Includes index.
Bibliography: p.
ISBN-13:978-1-4613-8927-9 (alk. paper)
1. Juvenile corrections—United States—Evaluation. 2. Juvenile delinquency—United States—restitution. I.Schneider, Anne L.
II. Title. III. Series.
HV9014.S323 1989
364.3′6′0973—dc20 89-11600

Printed on acid-free paper.

Typeset by David E. Seham Associates, Inc., Metuchen, New Jersey.

9 8 7 6 5 4 3 2

ISBN-13:978-1-4613-8927-9 e-ISBN-13:978-1-4613-8925-5
DOI: 10.1007/978-1-4613-8925-5

Contents

List of Figures

List of Tables

1
The Punishment Perspective

Introduction

Americans have an abiding faith in punishment. Deterrence theory holds that if punishment is sufficiently swift, certain, and severe, then behavior will change in predictable ways. When punishment does not work as expected, the underlying assumptions of the punishment model are rarely questioned; instead, remedies are sought through more punishment, delivered more rapidly, and with greater certainty.

The juvenile justice system traditionally has emphasized treatment rather than punishment, and has relied on probation, social services, and counseling programs for juvenile offenders. Skepticism about the effectiveness of treatment approaches in the 1960s and 1970s, however, undermined what had come to be known as the "medical" model of juvenile justice. Policy changes reflecting shifts toward more punishment-oriented policies for juveniles have been widely documented, including lowered age of jurisdiction for the adult court, increased waivers of juvenile cases to be heard in adult courts, increased penalties for juvenile crime, and greater reliance on detention and incarceration.

Concomitant with these changes, however, has been a much less publicized shift toward the use of restitution—in the form of monetary repayment to victims or symbolic repayment through community service. Although restitution is one of the most ancient responses to crime, it had not been used extensively in juvenile courts until the late 1970s. Reliance on restitution reflects a fundamentally different approach to juvenile crime, one that emphasizes holding juveniles accountable to victims and to the community for their offenses in a manner that is proportionate to the harm done and to the youth's level of responsibility for the harm.

This research was funded by the National Science Foundation Grant number SES-8520176. Data were collected under grants from the National Institute of Juvenile Justice, Office of Juvenile Justice and Delinquency Prevention, Washington, D.C.

All three sanctions—punishment, treatment, and restitution—are intended to reduce recidivism and juvenile crime. Yet, the actual effects of these sanctions on behavior are not well known, and even less is known about the perceptual mechanisms through which policy choices influence behavior.

Deterrence theory, in its simplest form, assumes that criminal or delinquent behavior can be reduced by increasing the certainty, severity, and celerity (speed) of punishment. Deterrence is a type of expected or subjective utility theory that assumes individuals weigh the benefits and costs of breaking the law by assessing the expected gain from the crime against the expected punishment that might be received, with the latter discounted as a function of time. Even if crime could be reduced by increasing the expected gain from legitimate activities through treatment, rehabilitation, or major changes in social conditions, these approaches are considered too indirect and expensive by advocates of deterrence, since the same effect can be achieved by increasing the certainty, severity, or celerity of punishment. From a deterrence perspective, punishment policies such as detention or incarceration are expected to be more effective than either probation or restitution because detention and incarceration are expected to be perceived as more severe punishment by would-be offenders.

Other theories of choice, however, suggest that decisions are governed more by heuristics—mental shortcuts, or rules of thumb—than by estimates of gains or losses, particularly when the actual results of behavior are difficult to predict. Uncertainty about the outcome of action makes it difficult or impossible for most individuals to adhere to the principles of strictly rational weighing of gains and losses as suggested by deterrece and other utility maximizing theories. Decision heuristic theories suggest that individuals adopt simple rules of thumb that guide behavior, and that many choices are better explained by a person's values, self-image, and the circumstances or context within which the decision emerges, than by an analysis of the actual benefits, costs, or risks involved.

Labeling theory rests on the assumption that punishment, or even nonpunitive interventions by the juvenile justice system, will stigmitize juveniles, damage self-esteem, increase the likelihood that the juvenile will identify with a "lawbreaking" self-image rather than a "good citizen" image, and interfere with the juvenile's ability to be successful in normal activities such as school or work. Labeling theory does not usually contain an explanation of the decision-making processes through which interventions shape the decisions to commit subsequent acts, but labeling theory is more consistent with a decision heuristics perspective than with one assuming strict rationality.

Equity theory, or accountability approaches such as restitution, also are more consistent with decision heuristics than with strict rationality. These perspectives hold that interventions should be proportionate to the harm done and to the level of culpability for the actions. The purpose of the intervention is to permit the offender to rectify the harm done, thereby restoring both the victim and offender to their rightful place in society. Some proponents of equity theory argue that there is an inherent tendency in individuals toward fairness and balance in social or political situations (Deutsch, 1985). Sanctions that are viewed as unfair, then, may help an offender rationalize subsequent offenses; whereas sanctions that permit individuals to repay victims and community, and that are viewed as fair, should be associated with reduced inclinations to reoffend.

Social control theory, as articulated by Hirschi (1969, 1986), also assumes that individuals weigh costs and benefits of alternative lifestyles. But the emphasis here is more on the benefits to be gained from conventional behavior, the likelihood of success in legitimate lifestyles, and commitment to the moral codes of society. Thus, the effectiveness of juvenile court interventions depends less on whether the sanction enhances perceptions of certainty and severity of punishment, and more on whether it improves the individual's capacity for success in law-abiding activities and strengthens the person's commitment to the moral codes of society. Probation should be a more effective approach than detention or incarceration because it should have greater potential for building the individual's capacity for law-abiding behavior. Restitution could have the same effect, particularly if it enhances the juveniles' ability to obtain and hold a job, encourages them to accept the responsibility for repaying victims, and demonstrates to the youths that they have the capacity to be successful in legitimate activities.

Purpose

The purpose of this book is to examine the perceptual mechanisms that link delinquency policy to changes in recidivism, and to seek explanations for why juveniles who have been exposed to numerous programs designed to reduce delinquency continue or discontinue their criminal activity. Perceptions of certainty and severity of punishment will be examined, along with the juvenile's sense of citizenship, perceptions of fairness, and feelings of remorse. The study will examine alternative policy responses to juvenile crime and the impact on perceptions as well as on subsequent delinquency. The intent is to understand the decision processes through which experiences in the juvenile justice system impact perceptions and how these, in turn, influence criminal activity.

The research emerges from a major national policy experiment funded by the Office of Juvenile Justice and the National Institute of Juvenile Justice. The experiment was designed to compare the effects of restitution against traditional sanctions of probation and incarceration and to explore the decision-making processes through which policy responses to crime influence subsequent behavior. Data for the study are from six juvenile courts in which youth were randomly assigned into restitution, incarceration, or probation programs.

An Overview

The results of the analysis may be profoundly disturbing to some, profoundly satisfying to others, and in either case there are substantial public policy implications. In six different cities in the United States, juvenile delinquents convicted of felonies and serious misdemeanor offenses, did not reduce their propensity to commit subsequent crimes as a function of their perceptions of the certainty or severity of punishment. In fact, the relationships sometimes were statistically significant in the wrong directions. Those who believed they would be punished more severely and those who perceived a higher likelihood of being caught professed a more marked intention of not committing crimes; but these juveniles actually committed more crimes during the two- to three-year followup period. In contrast, juveniles who had a greater sense of citizenship, as reflected in self-images as good, honest, law-abiding persons, and those who expressed more remorse for previous crimes, were substantially less likely to continue committing delinquent or criminal acts.

For the most chronic offenders in the study (those with six or more priors), there was a relationship between perceptions of punishment severity and reduced recidivism. However, the overwhelming evidence for all groups included in the research is that incarceration had no discernable effect on perceptions of certainty and severity of punishment. Instead incarceration and detention increased remorse, but also damaged the individual's self-image. These effects of punishment offset one another, leaving punishment policies with about the same results as less coercive programs such as restitution and probation.

Community-based restitution and work-service programs were more effective in reducing illegal behavior than traditional probation. The success of these programs, however, required that the courts adopt a programmatic approach to restitution, involving specific assistance to the juveniles in developing, implementing, and carrying out the restitution orders.

The findings may have considerable implications beyond the juvenile justice system. Public policies in all policy domains rely on policy tools that influence decisions and behavior of target populations. One of the most common policy tools is punishment or the threat of punishment, which is expected to have a deterrent effect. Policy failures in domains other than juvenile justice may be produced by overreliance on punishment in situations where it does not have the expected effect on behavior.

Organization of the Book

The remainder of the book is organized as follows.

Chapter 2 contains a review of previous research on deterrence and the competing perspectives that underly the use of restitution and probation.

Chapter 3 is a discussion of deterrence theory as a form of subjective expected utility theory and an examination of decision heuristics. This chapter closes with a decision-based model linking policy alternatives, perceptions, and recidivism.

Chapter 4 explains the methodology used in the research, including the field experiments that permit comparisons of restitution, probation, and incarceration. This chapter also includes an overview of all the data from the six experiments.

Chapter 5 presents results from the tests of the perceptual models of crime, and the efforts to explain or understand why perceptions of certainty and severity of punishment performed so poorly in predicting subsequent offenses.

Chapter 6 links experiences in the juvenile justice system to recidivism and demonstrates that (1) restitution programs were more effective in reducing offenses than traditional probation; (2) programmatic restitution, where there was an identifiable program with responsibility for assisting the juveniles in carrying out the requirements of the restitution orders, were more effective than ad hoc or unstructured approaches, where restitution was ordered but was not considered an integral part of the youth's program; and (3) incarceration and detention programs had about the same effects as restitution.

Chapter 7 links experiences to perceptions and perceptions to recidivism, revealing that detention and incarceration did not enhance perceptions of certainty or severity of punishment. and did not reduce recidivism to a greater extent than restitution programs. More severe punishments increased remorse, and this may explain why they have a suppression effect on recidivism, but they also damage the sense of citizenship and have other negative effects that leaves them with no net advantage over restitution.

Chapter 8 is a review of the theoretical and policy implications from the study, suggestions for the direction of future research, and reflections on the role of random experiments in producing knowledge about the outcomes of public policy initiatives.

2
Policy, Perceptions, and Criminal Behavior

The revival of modern deterrence theory in criminal justice began in the 1960s, and has enjoyed considerable popularity among the general public, political leaders, and in some academic circles. Deterrence theory fits nicely into the modern American view that individual behavior is driven mainly by incentives and that public policy can influence behavior most efficiently by manipulating the costs, benefits, and risks that adhere in particular decision contexts. Within the social sciences, deterrence theory is one of a broad group of theories based on common assumptions of utility maximization: individuals weigh the net utility of alternative actions and generally choose those from which they have the most to gain.

In spite of the obvious simplicity, reasonableness, and power of the theory, there are problems with its application. The chapter begins with the emergence of modern deterrence theory and concludes with studies of the effect of perceptions on crime and the effect of sanctions on perceptions.

General Deterrence Research

Aggregate Data Studies

Two of the earliest and most influential studies on deterrence were undertaken to identify the optimal level of public expenditures on crime control (Becker, 1968; Ehrlich, 1973). Becker, following the traditional economic approach, developed a model of social costs of crime that incorporated the cost of punishment to the offender and to society and the net social harm, defined as the total harm to society minus the gain to the offender from the crime itself.

Becker's article generated enormous controversy, most of it focused on his use of expected utility theory as an explanation for criminal behavior. Becker described his approach as follows (Becker, 1968, p. 177):

> This approach implies that there is a function relating the number of offenses to the probability of conviction, . . . to punishment if convicted, and to other vari-

ables such as the income available in legal and illegal activities, . . . and to willingness to commit an illegal act.

He proposed that utility theory should replace the "ad hoc concepts of differential association, anomie, and the like" commonly used in sociological approaches to the study of crime. Becker's conceptualization of expected utility theory was a flexible one, deviating in many respects from the narrow, profit-maximizing perspective sometimes used in economic applications of utility theory. He noted, for example, that utility theory "does not assume perfect knowledge, lightening-fast calculation, or any of the other caricatures of economic theory" (1968, p. 176). In spite of these caveats, his ideas ran counter to the strong inclinations in sociology, psychology, and political science that criminal behavior was produced by social conditions; individual personality traits; perceptions of gains, losses, and risks involving many values other than economic ones; or combinations of these that there were far more complex than envisioned in Becker's work.

Isaac Ehrlich's first study, published in 1973, operationalized much of Becker's framework. In three separate cross-sectional analyses (1940, 1950, and 1960) he found that the rate of felonies in the American states was positively related to variables representing the gain from crime and negatively related to the costs of crime—particularly the variables representing certainty of arrest. He extended the analysis to show that probability of arrest was negatively related to crime independent of incapacitation effects. After projecting the decreases in loss from crime that might be expected given an increase in spending on law enforcement, he concluded that expenditures were "less than optimal by a substantial amount" (Ehrlich, 1973, p. 565). Ehrlich estimated that a one percent increase in expenditures would produce a three percent drop in the crime rate.

This work has been continued by a number of scholars (Block & Heineke, 1975; Block & Lind, 1975; Brown & McDougal, 1978; Ehrlich, 1975; Wilson & Boland, 1978; for reviews see Blumstein, Cohen and Cook, 1980; Currie, 1985; Nagin, 1978; Tittle, 1985; Williams & Hawkins, 1986). Ehrlich's 1975 article found a deterrent effect for capital punishment using time series data from 1933 to 1969. Brown and McDougal (1978) argued that the utility function should be viewed even more more broadly than in previous studies, and they included estimates of several kinds of benefits expected from the crime itself, benefits from noncriminal behavior, and the costs of the crime. Their cross-sectional study of California cities indicated that all three factors were important in explaining differences (1978, p. 196). Wilson and Boland (1978, questioned Ehrlich's assertion that resources invested in criminal justice would necessarily increase arrest rates and reduce crime. They adopted a more strategic perspective in their cross-sectional analysis of 35 American cities, arguing that cities with more aggressive patrols would produce higher arrest rates for robberies, and that higher arrest rates for robbery would produce a decline in the robbery rate.

Nagin's (1978) review of 20 cross-sectional studies found 19 that concluded the certainty of punishment, usually measured as number of prisoners divided by number of index offenses, would reduce the crime rate. The conclusions drawn from aggregate data, cross-sectional studies, however, have been challenged on empirical, theoretical, and methodological grounds and the issue of whether there is a general deterrent effect is far from settled.

Contrary results have been reported by Jacob, Lineberry, Rich, and Heinz from a major time-series study of policy response to crime in nine American cities (Heinz, Jacob, & Lineberry, 1983; Jacob and Lineberry, 1982; Jacob & Rich, 1981) Their analysis revealed that increases in expenditures on crime had not stemmed the increase in crime but, in fact, appeared to accelerate it. This perverse finding was treated with understandable caution, but was explained as follows (Jacob & Lineberry, 1982, p. 127):

> It is as if legislators believed that the provision of more resources in the form of appropriations and personnel would suffice to solve the problem. But implementing agencies—lacking the technology to transform those resources into solutions—failed to achieve the hoped-for objectives.

They also disputed Wilson and Boland's results regarding the effect of aggressive patrols.

The findings of Jacob et al. cast some doubt on the efficacy of deterrence theory and on the wisdom of pursuing public policies that assume expenditures can be translated directly into desired results without substantial attention to the strategies incorporated in the policies. Jacob sharply disagrees with the use of utility theory as an explanation of criminal behavior:

> It [utility theory] implies that people who contemplate commiting a crime have a realistic perception of the probabilities of being sanctioned and of the severity of the sanction. . . . The little evidence we have . . . indicates that these perceptions are incorrect. . . . (1978:484).

He went on to argue that crime is the product of impulse or the result of "opportunity and need intersecting" rather than rational calculations of gains or losses.

Others (Gibbs, 1977; Tittle, 1985) contend that even if relationships between the deterrence variables and crime are in the expected direction, the explanation for the relationship at the individual level does not necessarily lie in calculations about the benefits and costs of crime, compared with the benefits and costs of law-abiding behavior. The effect of sanctions on behavior could be as easily attributed to the reaffirmation of the moral code of society. Thus, individuals restrain their behavior because they accept the social and moral norms of the society, not because of what they expect to gain or lose from the behavior.

The Methodological Critique

The major blow to the cross-sectional, aggregate data studies, however, comes from methodological rather than theoretical critiques. The contention that there was substantial scientific support for deterrence theory was thoroughly undermined by the persuasive National Academy of Sciences finding (Blumstein, Cohen, & Nagin, 1978) that the cross-sectional aggregate data studies, including those conducted by Becker, Ehrlich, Brown and McDougal, and dozens of others, were so fundamentally flawed that conclusions could not be drawn from them.

The cross-sectional aggregate data crime studies all relied upon reported crime rates, usually uniform crime reports, and all suffered from serious methodological problems. The most crucial is that variation in victim reporting of crimes, police recording of offenses, or prosecutorial use of plea bargaining will simultaneously reduce the apparent number of offenses and increase the apparent clearance rate as well as the apparent incarceration rate (Cook, 1980; Nagin, 1978).

Consider two cities with the same true certainty of punishment: one conviction per 100 actual crimes. Assume that all of the crimes in City A are reported, whereas only half the crimes in City B are reported. The reported crime rate in City B will be half that of city A, and the apparent certainty of punishment will be 1 in 50—twice that of City A. Thus, differences in citizen reporting among the units of analysis will produce spurious negative correlations between the apparent certainty of punishment and the reported crime rate. The same effect occurs if there are differences among the units of analysis in the extent of plea bargaining or in the proportion of reported crimes that police record in official data. Cross-sectional and time-series analyses both suffer from the problem, and statistical manipulations of the data will not be effective because the problem lies in the data.

As a result of the methodological problems, many criminal justice researchers have shifted from reliance on the cross-sectional or time-series aggregate data approaches to other methodologies, including evaluation research.

Macro-level Evaluation Research

Evaluations comparing different crime control programs have produced mixed results regarding the efficacy of punishment compared with other approaches. Although it is premature to proclaim any clear patterns, there is some indication that normal behavior, which carries little or no moral stigma, may be more readily reduced through sudden or dramatic increases in penalities or enforcement. Some recent research, for example, shows that increased penalities or enhanced enforcement have improved compliance with child-support laws (Lempert, 1982); reduced spouse abuse (Sherman & Berk, 1984); reduced accidents and deaths from drunk driving (Ross, McCleary, & Epperhein, 1982); and increased the number of persons wearing seat belts (Watson, 1986). Ross (1973) concluded that the British Road Safety Act had an initial strong deterrent effect on accidents, total casualities, serious injuries, and probability of death due to drunk driving, but the effect declined over time. Ross argued that discretionary decision making by police led to uneven enforcement and the perception that the probability of punishment was low. These perceptions, he contended, were reinforced on a regular basis as people learned they could drive while intoxicated and not get caught.

Williams et al. (1975) reported small effects on casualties in three states as an apparant result of changes in the legal minimum drinking age. Deutsch and Alt (1977) found a small deterrent effect for the Massachusetts gun control law, but others (Maltz & McCleary, 1977) disputed the finding on the ground that the effect was miniscule, if it existed at all, and of no practical or policy relevance.

Recidivism and Specific Deterrence

Studies of recidivism using individual-level data have been used to examine the specific deterrent effects of strategies for reducing recidivism rates of juvenile or adult offenders. In these studies, punishment-oriented programs are contrasted with treatment or diversion approaches, using recidivism rates or other indicators of program success.

Deterrence and Labeling

Labeling theory (Lemert, 1967; Thomas & Bishop, 1985) posits that secondary crime violations are primarily a product of social reactions to the initial crime. Through a complex process of identity formation, self-images, peer associations, and reinforcement, the official responses to crime actually perpetuate rather than reduce recidivism. Although one may be inclined to discount labeling theory at the outset since it purports to explain only secondary deviance, the theory argues that virtually everyone commits acts as a child for which they could be arrested and convicted of a crime. Thus, policy approaches that normalize these acts, at least for children and juveniles, may be more effective in preventing their reccurrence than policies that criminalize them (Klein, 1986). Informal adjustment of cases and diversion programs that do not involve the extension of social control are the most common examples.

Traditional probation programs are based upon what has become known as "medical" or treatment models of crime in which criminal or delinquent behavior is viewed as a "disease" from which one can be "cured" with the proper exposure to counseling, social services, and the like.

Direct comparisons of recidivism rates of persons who have been incarcerated and those who were placed on probation or diverted are rare and usually confounded by large differences in the seriousness of the offenders in the different programs. Since incarcerated populations are usually more serious offenders, they can generally be expected to have higher recidivism rates after release. The most widely quoted review of probation and other treatment-oriented programs, conducted by Lipset, Martinson, and Wilkes (1978) concluded that "nothing works," Studies reported by Palmer (1978) from a random-assignment experiment conducted within the California Youth Authority indicated that the less punishment-oriented programs, such as probation or early release, were more effective for first offenders than the more coercive programs. For more serious offenders, there were essentially no differences in the re-arrest rates between those on probation and those given more severe sanctions.

Murray and Cox, using a quasi-experimental design, studied recidivism rates of serious juvenile offenders in Chicago who were either incarcerated or placed on probation (Murray & Cox, 1979. Their analysis of suppression effects (i.e., the pre- and post-individual-level offense rates) showed that those in the incarceration programs experienced a dramatic decline in average re-arrest rates from 6.3 per month, pre, to 2.9 per month, post. A comparison group of juveniles who were on probation also showed suppression effects, but not as dramatic. Further, the more restrictive the probationary program, the greater the suppression effect. Some of the criticisms directed at the study (see Maltz & McCleary, 1977) probably are not warranted, such as the contention that the juveniles are simply aging out, because the study included controls for age. Other problems, such as the possibility that both groups are simply regressing to the mean, and the group with the higher preprogram rate will regress further, are not as simple to dispel.

A recent review by Garrett (1985) of more than 100 residential programs for juvenile offenders compared the success rates of persons who experienced the normal residential program with those participating in special treatment programs. The latter showed an overall small but positive effect on recidivism rates, with life skills programs, such as outward bound and vocational training, being the most effective. Analysis of the intensive treatment-oriented probation programs, New Pride, showed no differences in recidivism rates compared with traditional dispositions for high-rate juvenile offenders.

Research on status offenders provides some support for using less intrusive interventions with these types of nonserious offenders. Kobrin and Klein (1982) found that the deinstitutionalization programs that relied heavily on counseling and social service perspectives, even when they purportedly were diverting juveniles, had a small but detectable increase in recidivism. Klein (1986) reported a small but interesting relationship between positive self-images and lower recidivism rates among status offenders. Schneider (1982) examined studies that attempted to compare recidivism rates of status offenders who had experienced detention with those who had not. Two thirds of these studies showed no recidivism differences of greater than five percentage points between the groups and the other third were divided evenly between studies showing that diversion was more effective and those showing that it was less effective.

One of the major problems in this literature is lack of information about the nature of the intervention itself, and the strategy it used to change behavior. Gendreau and Ross, in a particularly impressive review of program strategies, document that there are numerous rehabilitative strategies that have had major impacts on recidivism rates, and that these often outperform the more coercive, punishment-oriented approaches (Gendreau & Ross, 1981, 1987; see also Cullen & Gendreau, 1989). Nevertheless, conclusions are difficult to draw from this literature. The effect of probation and incarceration on recidivism varies from one study to another, and patterns are difficult to find.

Restitution Programs

Most direct comparisons of restitution programs with other dispositions indicate that restitution produces lower recidivism rates. The first reported restitution study compared a group of adult parolees who had been released from prison with the expectation that they would pay restitution to their victims with a matched group who served out their full terms before being released (Heinz, Hudson, & Galaway, 1976). This study concluded that those in the restitution groups had fewer reconvictions. Similar positive effects were reported by Hudson and Chesney (1978) in a two-year followup of adult offenders released from the Minnesota Restitution Center. However, Bonta (1983) found that persons in an adult restitution program had higher recidivism rates than those in a comparison group, but the difference was small and not statistically significant. In that study, offenders in both groups were in job programs; some were required to pay restitution and others were not. This study was confounded by the fact that those in the restitution program were more serious offenders.

The first test of restitution and recidivism of juveniles was reported by Wax (1977), who found no differences but observed that restitution had positive effects on some psychological tests. The size of the sample in this study was so small (36) that the possibility of finding an impact, even if one existed, was quite low. The second study (Guedalia, 1979) examined 250 juvenile offenders from Tulsa county and found that persons who had more contacts with victims and lower restitution orders were less likely to reoffend. Cannon and Stanford (1981) found a 19 percent rearrest rate among restitution cases over a six-month time period, compared with a 24 percent rate for the nonrestitution group. Hofford (1981) reported an 18 percent recidivism rate for youths in the restitution program, compared with a 30 percent rate for those on regular probation. In the last two studies, no data were reported on the comparative seriousness of the offenders in the studies.

These results are instructive, but as is the case with much field research, serious methodological problems confound the studies, making it necessary to rely more heavily on replication than on the results of any one study. With the exception of Wax's study and the adult study by Heinz et al., none had a satisfactory degree of equivalence between the comparison group and the recidivism group, and efforts to control for differences statistically were not undertaken.

Methodological Issues

The evaluation studies that examine the effect of policies on recidivism rates do not suffer from the same kinds of methodological problems inherent in the cross-sectional aggregate date analysis. In both types of studies, however, the nature of the effect has to be inferred based upon a relationship between an intervention and an outcome. If the analyst assumes the intervention is punishment, rather than treatment and if recidivism is reduced, then the explanation could be that programs influence perceptions of certainty and severity of punishment. But the linkage could involve other mechanisms, such as an enhanced sensitivity to the impact of crime on victims or greater recognition of the importance of adhering to basic norms of society. Further, the analyst must assume that the program is punishment or treatment and this is not always a simple task. There is nothing inherent about probation that places it in one category rather than another. Many professionals in the field of juvenile justice contend that institutions deliver treatment rather than punishment.

The missing link in this research is perceptions. Whether the intervention is treatment or punishment should be ascertained from the perspective of the recipient. When relationships are found between interventions and recidivism, the perceptual linkage needs to be explored. Proponents of punishment often argue that if the intervention has not worked, then the remedy is to increase the severity, certainty, or celerity of punishment. The logic is straightforward: if punishment does not work, the reason must be that those to whom it is administered did not perceive it as punishment. When told that incarcerated criminals, upon release, tend to accelerate their crime patterns, some public officials are more inclined to believe that the prison was a country club than they are to believe that punishment is not effective in changing behavior. Proponents of treatment programs often react in a similar manner: if the treatment did not work, it was because the program was not sufficiently intense or was not of sufficient duration. The suggested remedy is to intensify the treatment or increase its duration.

Perceptions of Legal Sanctions

Most of the studies relating perceptions to criminal behavior have focused on the deterrence variables of perceived certainty and severity of punishment. These studies usually rely on survey research of general population samples or students. Questions are asked about the individual's perception of the likelihood of getting caught and the severity of punishment, if caught. Most studies have relied on self-reported crime or intentions to commit crimes as the dependent variable.

One-Wave Perceptual Research

The first-generation studies were all based on one-shot surveys without subsequent offense data, rather than panel surveys, or studies with followup information. Thus, perceptions of certainty and severity were correlated with self-reported criminal behavior that had occurred during the past year (or over the lifetime of the respondent). This methodology reversed the temporal order of interest in the study—a problem recognized by the researchers but not assumed to be sufficiently serious to invalidate the results. Others, recognizing the problem of temporal order, correlated perceptions of certainty and severity with self-reported intentions of committing or not committing crimes in the future.

Using methodologies with the reversed temporal order or using intentions rather than self-reported delinquency, most of the research findings echoed those of the aggregate studies: there was support for a relationship between certainty of punishment and self-reported or intended criminal or delinquent acts but most did not find support for a relationship between perceptions of the severity of punishment and illegal behavior.

Waldo and Chiricos (1972) could not detect a relationship between perceived severity of punishment and self-reported marijuanna smoking on theft although perceived risk (certainty) was associated with lower levels on both. Teevan (1976) found that certainty was related to self-reported marijuanna use and shoplifting but that perceived severity was not. He reported an interaction effect similar to that suggested by Tittle (1969) in which severity became important only when certainty was sufficiently high to justify concern. Hollinger and Clark (1983) found that both perceived certainty and severity influenced the extent of self-reported employee theft and that there were no interaction effects. Grasmick and Bryjack (1980), in one of the more thoughtful and careful analyses, found that both perceived certainty and severity had an independent impact on self-reported offenses as well as an interaction effect similar to that reported by Teevan.

The perceptual studies also have examined whether formal or informal sanctions were better inhibitors of illegal behavior among juveniles. And several researchers have tested the importance of moral commitment or other ethical beliefs in reducing illegal actions. The results of this research generally suggest that all are important (Grasmick & Appleton, 1977; Grasmick & Green, 1980; Teevan, 1976), although, as before, the reversal of the temporal order calls these findings into question. Grasmick and Green (1980) suggested that the effects are additive and account for about 40 percent of the variance in self-reported illegal behavior.

Unfortunately, as with the cross-sectional studies, the methodological problems now appear to be more serious than originally believed. Recent publication of research by Paternoster, Saltzman, Chiricos, and Waldo (1982), and Paternoster, Saltzman, Waldo, and Chiricos (1983) and by Piliavin, Thornton, Gartner, and Matsueda (1986) demonstrated with panel data that relationships between perceived certainty and self-reported crime—when measured at the same point in time—probably reflect the effect of crime experience on perceptions rather than the effect of perceptions on criminal behavior. Thus, although the theoretical advances from this work are substantial, the empirical evidence is weak.

Second Generation Perceptual Research

Following the initial Paternoster report, a second generation of perceptual studies was initiated. At this writing, there have been at least five studies of perceptions and crime that have used the proper temporal order: perceptions were measured in interviews at time 1 and follow-up interviews or the collection of subsequent official data was used to measure crime and delinquent behavior. These studies have shown either no support for deterrence theory or weak support, depending on one's interpretation of the results (see Williams & Hawkins, 1986, for a review).

Paternoster et al. (1982, 1983) found bivariate negative relationships between perceptions of certainty and subsequent minor crimes in samples of college students, but they found that these effects were reduced substantially and did not reach the 0.05 signficiance level when variables representing moral commitment and social disapproval were included in the model. They concluded that moral commitment and informal sanctions were important but that classical deterrence theory was not supported by their findings. Virtually the same conclusions were reached by Minor and Harry (1982), whose research also was conducted using college students. The relationships between certainty of sanctions and subsequent delinquency were in the expected direction but failed to reach statistical significance at the 0.05 level.

Bishop (1984) found statistically significant effects on subsequent delinquent behavior in a large sample of junior-high and high-school students for perceptions of legal sanctions, commitment to moral norms, and perceptions of informal sanctions. The path coefficients in her work were of about the same magnitude as in the other two studies, but with the larger sample they reached the 0.05 significance level.

It is possible, of course, that deterrence works through perceptions of moral sanctions and social disapproval. Axelrod (1986), for example, has developed a theory of metanorms that indicates moral norms and social disapproval may follow and be reinforced by official sanctions. Thus, policies based on punishment may be effective in controlling crime even if perceptions of certainty and severity are not associated with subsequent criminality.

Piliavin et al. (1986), in one of the most comprehensive and careful studies of subjective utility theory to date, found that perceptions of risk of formal and personal sanctions failed to make a difference in explaining subsequent criminal behavior in a large sample of adults and juveniles involved in publically supported work programs. However, both the perceptions of potential gain from crime and the self-reported availability of crime opportunities had a weak but important and consistent relationship to subsequent crime. They drew the following conclusion:

> We find evidence supporting the opportunity and reward component of the rational choice model of crime, but no evidence supporting the risk component. . . . The rational choice model may oversimplify the cognitive process behind criminality. What may be needed is a more complex model that relaxes some of the stringent assumptions of the strict rational choice approach. (1986, p. 115)

The "opportunity" variable was not actually incorporated in the formal statement of their rational choice model, and probably is better interpreted as part of the predecision processes that lead up to consideration of criminal behavior. Opportunities for crime, in fact, are ever-present for all individuals. It is the seeking out of specific opportunities or the recognition of an opportunity, combined with the capacity to commit crime (i.e., resources, strength, knowledge), that is important. Further, it must be noted that Piliavan et al. had a very large sample and even the relationships that were statistically significant were weak. Their research, however, is of considerable importance for public policy because it demonstrates the weakness of deterrence theory.

In the fifth study, Lanza-Kaduce (1988) found no relationship between perceptions of certainty or severity and self-reported drunk driving among college students. Experiences with being stopped by the police also had no effect. Instead, the best explanatory variable was the belief that drinking while driving was wrong.

Sanctions and Perceptions

Deterrence and labeling perspectives both assume that sanctions influence perceptions, although they offer opposite conclusions about the implications of those effects.

Thomas and Bishop (1984) reported that involvement in delinquent behavior reduced perceptions of the certainty of punishment, but neither formal nor informal sanctions influenced perceptions of risk. Formal sanctions, however, had a small, negative, effect on self-image. The authors concluded that neither the deterrent nor the labeling perspective received much support in their data:

> . . . labeling theorists attribute far more significance to sanctions imposed by formal or quasi-formal agents of social control than is attributed to them by those who are sanctioned. Deterrence theorists seem even more detached from the world in which most of the rest of us live. (Thomas & Bishop, 1984, p. 1244)

On the other hand, Bridges and Stone (1986) interviewed 550 convicted felons serving time in a federal prison and found that the extent of prior punishment had essentially no effect on perceived threat of punishment, with threat measured as estimated likelihood of arrest for each of three different types of crimes. Elaboration of the analysis, however, showed that naive offenders were influenced by their prior experiences with punishment, whereas experienced offenders were not. In fact, those who had more prior experience with punishment were more approving of crime which, in turn, was associated with lower perceptions of the threat of punishment. The authors conclude that (p. 231)

> For experienced offenders, punishment may be expected to have little or no deterrent effect on criminal recidivism because it has limited impact on the perceived threat of punishment. . . . Among offenders with long histories of crime, apprehension and punishment may be accepted as hazards that are inconsequential when compared with the potential benefits of crime.

Unresolved Issues

These second-generation studies are very important, but there are a host of issues unresolved. The findings are not consistent, and it is not clear whether perceptions of certainty and severity of punishment are related to recidivism, or whether commitment to norms or fear of informal sanctions actually are the controlling factors. Further, without a better understanding of how sanctions influence perceptions, self-image, and commitment to social norms, it is not clear whether policy shifts toward more coercive, or less coercive, interventions will produce the desired effects.

The mixed empirical results also thwart advances in theory. Although many scholars are now willing to acknowledge that criminals may engage in reasoned behavior and pay some heed to rewards and punishments, most are not at all comfortable with simplistic models of utility maximization (see Cornish & Clarke, 1986). Substantial theoretical advances have been made recently, however, by incoporating more explicit models of decision making that recognize the limits of rationality (Cornish & Clark, 1986).

The research reported in this book is intended to extend the recent work linking policy, perceptions, and behavior and to seek explanations for the findings by careful probing of the decision processes through which different sanctioning experiences influence perceptions and subsequent recidivism. In addition, this research extends the studies to a different and very important population.

The second-generation studies thus far have been conducted mainly with high-school and college students, many of whom have never committed any nontrivial crimes, or with young adults in work programs, most of whom also have not committed crimes. Thus, the types of people and crimes for which the findings might be important are still quite limited. In addition, since the studies have not been undertaken with court-referred persons, there is no way to examine the impact of court intervention on perception or subsequent criminal behavior. And, finally, a key issue involves whether the weak relationships between perceptions of certainty and subsequent behavior can be found with any consistency and whether perceptions of severity are related to subsequent crime. Policy makers may believe it is less costly to increase the severity of penalties than to increase the probability of arrest, conviction, and actual receipt of a penalty. Thus, it is particularly important to examine empirical evidence about both the effects of sanctions and the mechanisms through which these effects are produced.

3
Rational Choice and Decision Heuristics

Deterrence and Subjective Expected Utility Theory

Deterrence is best understood as a type of subjective or expected utility theory. Subjective utility theory assumes that individuals are rational decision makers in that they select among options on the basis of perceived net utility where utility is a function of benefits, costs, and probabilities associated with each. This can be expressed as follows:

$$Uc = [Bq - [(Cp)(1/t)]] - [Dr - [(Es) * 1/t]]$$

where Uc = the individual's expected net utility from the crime;
B = expected gain from the crime;
q = subjective probability of completing the crime and realizing the gain from it;
C = expected punishment cost if caught;
p = subjective probability of being caught;
t = time to punishment, if caught;
D = expected gain from noncrime;
r = subjective probability of gain;
E = expected cost of noncrime;
s = subjective probability of incurring the cost.

Pilivian (1986) used a similar formulation, as have Ehrlich (1975), Phillips and Votey (1981), Shapiro and Votey (1984), and numerous others.

Wilson and Herrnstein (1985) proposed a more complex theory of crime resting upon the fundamental premise that behavior is driven by choices that, in turn, are determined by perceptions of consequences, but the process is exceptionally complex and can be expected to differ from one individual to another. Their theory incorporates four major concepts: the net reward or certainty of reward for noncrime compared to crime; the probabilities of receiving the rewards for crime or noncrime; the delay between the crime (or noncrime) and the reinforcement or penalties for it; and the individual's propensity for impulsiveness. Their conception of "reward" is quite broad-based including all tangible or intangible benefits or costs that might be important to the individual. Impulsiveness refers to how the individual discounts time. Those who discount time steeply (i.e., are highly impulsive) will discount the value of punishment and its certainty as both of these are delayed negative effects in comparison with the immediacy of the gains from the criminal act itself. Further, their theory emphasizes that the strength of a particular behavior, vis a vis all behavior, depends upon the strength of the net rewards for that behavior, vis a vis all behavior. The importance of other variables, they argue, may well outweigh the deterrence variables (Wilson & Herrnstein, 1985; p. 508):

> Among the many who experiment with crime and the few who persist in it, the contingencies of reinforcements and punishments will have an effect on the rate at which they offend, but it may be less than the effect obtained by the presence or absence of internalized restraints on crime, notably conscience and a desire for the good opinion of others.

Even though internalized or "substantive" states may be more important than contingent incentive structures, Wilson and Herrnstein argue that the former are also much more difficult to influence through legitimate use of public policy. They also point out, as others have, that marginal differences in the level of punishment or its certainty may not be nearly as important as the fact that there is any penalty at all for particular acts. Even though Wilson and Herrnstein clearly recognize the limitations of deterrence, they remain confident that it will have some effect (1985, p. 397):

> To increase the expected disutility of crime for people in general, society must increase either the speed, the certainty, or the severity of punishment, or some combination of all three.

Most proponents of deterrence theory believe that net utility is the controlling concept and it does not matter whether utility is altered through negative or positive incentives. Wilson and Herrnstein, for example, argue for the basic commonality of positive and negative inducements (1985, p. 376):

> If we try to change the likelihood of an individual's committing a crime by increasing the risk of imprisonment, psychologically we are not doing anything very different from trying to lower the crime rate by increasing the attractiveness of legitimate work; in both cases, we are trying to increase the expected value of noncrime relative to crime.

A Critique

Although subjective utility theory often is used as a point of departure for studies of deterrence as well as studies of choice and decisions in many contexts, its value as a descriptive or predictive theory of behavior under conditions of uncertainty is often found lacking. Even those who wish to develop cognitive or information-processing theories of criminal behavior are not usually willing to rely upon the assumptions of subjective or expective utility theory. The authors in Cornish and Clarke's recent book, *The Reasoning Criminal,* for example, uniformly reject the assumptions of strict rationality that underly deterrence theory.

There are several problems with the formal models of choice upon which subjective or expected utility theory rests.

First, experimental research shows repeatedly that individuals, under conditions of uncertainty, often are not utility maximizers but employ less complex strategies in arriving at choices (Edwards, 1955; Lichtenstein, Slovic, 1971). Edwards demonstrated in a series of experiments that individuals do not choose gambles in accordance with the principles of expected utility theory when outcomes are uncertain but based upon known probabilities. Lichtenstein et al. showed in numerous experimental studies during the 1970s that expected utility was almost worthless as a predictor of choice in selecting gambles to maximize earnings even when probabilities were known and the concepts were carefully explained to the subjects (see Slovic, Fischoff, & Lichtenstein, 1977; Wright, 1984, for comprehensive reviews).

Second, individuals make numerous errors in judging the probability of events; hence their ability to act as utility maximizers in real-world situations is seriously compromised (Kahneman, Slovic, & Tversky, 1982).

Third, some behaviors are better accounted for by theories based upon an individual's perception of what is right or wrong or ethical or a part of ones duties or by perceptions of group interest or by a spirit of altruism than by their perceptions of personal gain (Deutsch, 1985; Orbell, Peregrine & Simmons, 1984; Rapoport. 1985).

Fourth, utility theory deals only with the weighing of alternatives and does not address the prechoice processes through which situations are interpreted and alternatives for action created. Thus, the values (benefits and costs) that individuals believe are associated with a particular problem situation may differ enormously since the individuals may frame the problem in different terms.

Most social and behavioral scientists who study individual choice from an empirical perspective have modified the simple versions of subjective utility theory by incorporating other variables into the benefits or costs portions of the theory and most do not assume that individuals incorporate perceptions of risk in the multiplicative model implied by subjective utility theory. Many researchers have found that individuals often produce public goods when utility theory predicts that they will not do so or that they act in concert with group interests or with the public interest rather than their own narrowly defined self-interest when confronted with collective decision situations (Meehl, 1977; Van DeKraft, Orbell, & Dawes, 1983). There is considerable evidence that not all behavior is motivated by perceptions of gains and losses of tangible valued items; many intangible values such as individualism, equality, doing what is right or being fair are viewed as important in understanding individual decisions and choice (Deutsch, 1985; Rawles, 1971; Wildavsky, 1987) When Riker and Ordeshook, for example, found that the simple versions of subjective utility theory could not explain voting behavior, they altered the formula to incorporate a variable called "citizens duty." Individuals may not choose an alternative solely because of what will be produced for themselves or others; rather, their behavior may be grounded in nonutilitarian cultural principles. Some versions of justice theory are distinctly nonutilitarian in the sense that they suggest individuals are not motivated by the prospect of future consequences but act in accordance with basic principles regardless of the future states that might be forthcoming.

Modifying Rational Choice Theory

There are different ways of coping with these problems, both theoretically and empirically. One could argue, as Axelrod has, that norms are important in individual decision processes, but that these actually arise from an underlying calculation of costs, benefits, and probabilities even though at any given point in time they serve as powerful motivations for behavior that may appear to be independent of considerations of personal gain. Rapoport (1985) argued that "individuals have utilties that determine their behavior" but he concluded that these utilities "are associated with aspects of behavior, such as altruism, social norms, and moral conventions, other than the external payoffs" (p. 153). Margolis (1982) has developed a formal modification of utility theory, which takes into account the fact "that people make contributions to what they perceive as the public interest . . . in contexts where the return to the individual appears inconsequential and the effect on society is microscopic" (1982, p. 2).

Many adaptations of utility theory build from the work of Herbert Simon and psychologists who have experimented with decision making under conditions of uncertainty and risk (Kahneman, Tversky, and Slovic, 1982; Slovic, Fischoff, & Lichtenstein, 1977). In these theories, individuals make choices that are not consistent with the predictions from expected utility theory because they rely on decision heuristics—that is, short cuts or rules of thumb used to simplify judgment tasks "to make them tractable for the kind of mind that people happen to have" (Kahneman, Slovic, & Tversky, 1982, p. xii).

A Decision Heuristics Approach

If individuals do not always follow the prescriptions of subjective utility theory, then there are good reasons to believe that deterrence variables, certainty, severity, and celerity of punishment, will not be particularly good predictors of subsequent behavior, or that these variables may be highly contingent, with effects that are observable only under certain circumstances. Thus, it will be useful to develop a model of individual decisions about illegal behavior that incorporates perceptions of certainty and severity of punishment, but one that modifies subjective utility theory by examining the types of decision heuristics that produce deviations from it.

Decision Heuristics

Decision heuristics are shortcuts or mental strategies that are used to make choices but do not conform to the prescriptions of subjective utility theory. A decision heuristics approach does not address only the choice among already-developed alternatives, as is the case with subjective expected utility theory, but examines the entire process through which problems are identified, alternatives designed, and choices made. This process is driven by contextual features, values, opportunities, and pure happenstance, as well as by perceptions of rewards and punishment. The decision process itself involves four interactive parts:

1. Framing. Framing refers to the definition of the situation or problem confronting the individual. The way in which the problem is framed has substantial implications for the response.
2. Search. Search involves scrutiny of large stores of information stored in memory to identify ideas or approaches to the problem.
3. Crafting. Crafting refers to the means/ends reasoning, simulations, and other strategies used to design a possible course of action.
4. Choice. The choice of a course of action may not be based upon selection from among alternatives, but may involve choosing the only alternative that has been identified.

A decision heuristics approach differs from traditional versions of subjective or expected utility theory in that it recognizes the limits in cognitive reasoning and seeks to understand how decisions are actually made. It recognizes that many decisions are made under conditions of uncertainty, and that individuals may not be able to estimate probabilities accurately, even when there are objective estimates available. It recognizes that individuals frame situations differently, and there will be considerable variance in the values people believe exist in a particular situation. Values, experiences, opportunities, and happenstance are important in understanding how choices emerge. Shortcuts and rules of thumb for decision making imply that values and self-identification may be better predictors than estimates of gains and losses, particularly under conditions of uncertainty. In some contexts, core or peripheral values may largely determine how the person defines the problem, where they search for ideas about courses of action, and the actions actually taken.

The decision heuristics perspective also recognizes that individuals differ in the way they arrive at decisions, and that most persons do not combine benefits, costs, and risks in the multiplicative fashion envisioned by subjective expected utility theory (Carroll, 1978; Carroll & Weaver, 1986; Wright, 1984). Further, there may be threshold effects so that unless the certainty of punishment is beyond some threshold level, the severity of punishment is not relevant (Tittle, 1980). Similarly, unless the sanctions used by the court are viewed as unpleasant, the certainty of receiving them may not be relevant. Finally, a decision heuristics perspective suggests considerable variance in decision-making process, based upon context. The same person will use different heuristics from one situation to another or perhaps even from one time period to another when dealing with the same phenomenon. Thus, it is not surprising that individuals commonly deviate from the prescriptions of subjective expected utility theory, and it is not surprising to find, within criminal and juvenile justice, that perceptions of certainty and severity of punishment are not strongly related (or perhaps not related at all) to the level of subsequent activity.

The key issue, then, in developing a decision heuristics theory relating policy, perceptions, and criminal behavior is to search for patterns in the heuristics employed and to identify characteristics of persons or situations associated with differing decision-making styles.

Several heuristics can be inferred from the criminal and juvenile justice literature. Indeed, a number of current theoretical perspectives, including deterrence, labeling, and normative approaches can be reconceptualized in a decision heuristics framework, thereby integrating the perspectives rather than treating them as competing theoretical frameworks. Different variables may be important in different contexts, or for different individuals.

One of the potentially most important decision heuristics involves the reliance on moral values and fundamental principles of right and wrong. It is apparent that most individuals have long-standing moral commitments that preclude them from engaging in many criminal activities, particularly robberies, burglaries, assaults with weapons, and the like. These persons may not recognize criminal opportunities when they are presented. Thus, they do not frame situations in such a way that will lead to further consideration of an illegal act. Their search for ideas on how to approach a problem may not bring to conscious attention any options that are illegal. On the other hand, fewer persons may exhibit similar kinds of moral commitments regarding obedience to speeding laws, driving while intoxicated, wearing seat belts, or cheating on income taxes. The decision process through which a person determines how fast to drive or whether to wear a seat belt almost certainly will bring to conscious attention a choice that is illegal. And, if a choice is considered, it is more likely to be chosen than if it was never considered at all. Hence, basic beliefs that crime is wrong, or that certain kinds of crime are wrong, may be related to law-abiding behavior because these beliefs screen out recognition of crime opportunities and because these beliefs truncate the decision process before the individual estimates what might be gained or lost from the crime itself. Many have suggested that legal sanctions may influence crime primarily through their confirmation of basic moral principles of society, rather than through fear (Gibbs, 1977; Silberman, 1976; Williams & Hawkins, 1986).

If reliance on moral principles is a factor that makes crime less attractive for some people, then individuals who do not adhere strongly to a set of basic moral or legal values may be more inclined to frame situations in such a way that the crime opportunity is apparent, and they may be more likely to evaluate these opportunities on some basis other than their moral correctness, possibly by assessing the benefits and risk. Hence, persons without strong moral principles may be influenced more by the certainty or severity of sanctions, than are persons without such principles. Applying the same logic, it is reasonable to believe that certain types of crimes—those for which there is little or no moral condemnation—will be more sensitive to deterrent effects of certainty and severity of punishment.

It is also possible that certain types of legal sanctions—restitution, for example—with its emphasis on accountability, responsibility, and justice, may increase commitment to basic moral values, whereas other traditional sanctions may not. Adjudicated offenders who believe their sanctions were fair and just may be less able to rationalize subsequent offenses, thereby producing a linkage between fairness and reduced recidivism (Deutsch, 1985). In a similar way, proponents of equity theory would argue that offenders who feel remorse for their crime and believe the victims did not deserve to be victimized will be less able to rationalize future offenses (Deutsch, 1985).

Another mental shortcut that might undermine the ability of an individual to accurately assess the utility of crime is suggested by labeling theory and the more general theories of self-image developed in psychology and sociology. Specifically, labeling theory contends that the actions taken by authorities confer labels on individuals—such as criminal, mentally ill, delinquent, and so forth. Individuals who accept the validity of these labels may make decisions and behave in a way consistent with the label itself (Gove, 1980; Tittle, 1980).

This is a simple decision strategy. Those who view themselves as honest, law-abiding citizens eschew most crime opportunities because they are not the type of people who commit crimes. They may not even recognize crime opportunities. Those who view themselves as law breakers would be more inclined to recognize opportunities, they may have a greater capacity to commit crimes, and they may evaluate the crime opportunity on its own merits—for example, benefits and risks of apprehension compared with perceptions of possible gains. Perceptions of how one is viewed by others could have substantially the same effect. Those who believe others think of them as law-abiding persons could rely simply on this expectation of others to forego crime, whereas those who think others view them as law breakers might rely simply on this perception or they might—as mentioned earlier—evaluate the situation in terms of the costs and benefits involved. This leads to a proposition similar to that suggested earlier: individuals who adopt positive self-labels as honest, law-abiding citizens may not evaluate crime opportunities on the basis of the deterrence variables, but those who adopt self-images as persons who break laws, disregard rules, and are dishonest, may be more sensitive to the costs, benefits, and risks presented by specific crime situations.

Experimental studies of decision processes suggest several other deviations from subjective utility theory that are of interest here. Carroll (1978) found that most juveniles who evaluated the attractiveness of various hypothetical criminal opportunities did not combine benefits, costs, and probabilities in either an additive or multiplicative model. Rather, most of them concentrated on only one of these dimensions. More than half, in fact, apparently rated the attractiveness of the opportunity solely in terms of the value to be gained, disregarding the probability of gaining it, the severity of the punishment if caught, and the likelihood of being caught.

Carroll's work echoes a sentiment commonly heard from probation officers and others who deal with juvenile delinquents or adult criminals: there is no one theory of criminal behavior and no one route to a criminal lifestyle. It is not entirely clear why social scientists expect individuals to follow a common decision-making pattern when, in introspective examination of our own decisions, we are quite aware of several different ways of seeking and combining information.

Recent interest in rational choice theory by criminologists rejects the formal models, such as subjective expected utility theory, in favor of more loosely structured information processing theories (Carrol & Weaver, 1986; Cook, 1986; 1986 Feeney,). One of the most important insights from this perspective is that decisions to adopt a criminal lifestyle are fundamentally different than decisions about when and where a particular crime will be committed. Formal models of expected utility theory are more appropriate for the latter than the former. Decisions about lifestyle are not made from moment to moment, but evolve over a period of time and are closely tied to the concepts of self-image already discussed.

Threshold effects also are important. Slovic (1967) found that there was a critical probability threshold below which individuals tended to ignore entirely the possibility of even very large losses. This sounds quite similar to Tittle's finding that there may be a critical level of certainty that must exist before the severity of punishment becomes relevant to the potential offender.

Laboratory experimental research almost universally supports the contention that behavior can be altered radically by punishment, but there are several conditions that must be met. Moffitt's (1983) review of the psychological studies suggests that behavioral change is a direct function of intensity (severity) of punishment, the extent of temporal delay, the absence of rewards for the behavior (i.e., the absence of immediate gratifications as a result of the criminal act), the consistency of punishment (i.e., the proportion of times that, when the act is committed, the punishment is administered), and the availability of behavior that will provide the same rewards being forsaken by the extinction of the punished behavior.

These findings reinforce the idea that perceptions of certainty, severity, and celerity should be important deterrents but they also call attention to other concepts and to the context itself. The immediate benefit from the crime act itself may be far more important than generally recognized. These benefits range from actual monetary gain to subjective benefits such as the fun, excitement, thrill, or social rewards received. A second implication is that an alternative behavior needs to be provided that will replace the rewards forsaken if the individual foregoes the criminal activity. It is important to recognize that in a real-world rather than a laboratory setting, the agents administering the sanction are not in control of the reward systems in other parts of the youth's environment—such as school, friends, work associates, and so forth. Of the dispositions used in juvenile court, only restitution—with its emphasis on work programs and community service—provides a true alternative behavior. Further, it is quite reasonable to acknowledge the contention held by labeling theorists that public and social perceptions of the youth who commits a delinquent act are affected by the extent of punishment as is the youth's self-perception. For these reasons, severe or prolonged punishment may foreclose the possibility of engaging in law-abiding behavior and produce a situation in which delinquents associate primarily with each other and frequently engage in quasi-legal or illegal activities because they are systematically excluded from conventional activities that produce the type of social bonding that Hirschi (1969) and most theorists believe is critical to avoid criminality.

The Decision Model

The decision model used in this study (see Figure 3.1) proposes that experiences in the juvenile system influence perceptions, including certainty, severity, good-citizen self-image, fairness of the sanction, and remorse. Experiences include both the type of program provided the youth and his or her ability to comply successfully with the program demands. Perceptions are expected to influence intentions to commit delinquent acts and the actual commission of subsequent crimes. A number of control variables will be included in the model, including the number of priors, age, race, and sex. Policy interventions also may influence the youth's school and job status, either of which also could influence subsequent offenses.

Punishment, particularly detention and incarceration, may impact per-

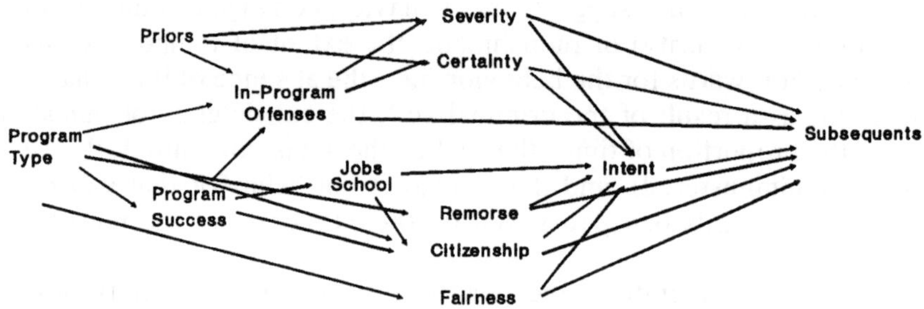

FIGURE 3.1. The Decision Model. (To avoid cluttering the diagram, not all linkages are shown.)

ceptions of certainty and severity in such a way as to deter future criminal behavior for some youths but these effects may be reduced or reversed due to the labeling effects. Probation may also influence perceptions of the certainty or severity of punishment but it, too, may have labeling effects. On the other hand, effective counseling in a probation setting might improve self-image or increase remorse. Restitution, which was administered by formal restitution programs for the juveniles in this study, differs from the traditional *parens patriae* philosophy of the court. As practiced by the programs from which these data were drawn, restitution was intended to hold youths accountable for their crimes and to impart to them an understanding of the consequences of criminal behavior of victims and for society.

Restitution differs fundamentally from other approaches in that it requires concrete action on the part of the youth from the point of disposition to release from court jurisdiction. Restitution has a more tangible measure of success in that juveniles who find employment and begin making payments to the victims, or who obtain community service positions, are working on a regular basis and have a tangible product to show for their efforts. As each payment is made, or each community service hour worked, there is a tangible action to be rewarded. Juveniles who successfully complete restitution have accomplished something that would not otherwise have been done, whereas juveniles who successfully complete probation or incarceration have only avoided doing those things that they were not supposed to do in the first place. The work experience itself could have a positive effect on the juvenile by influencing the youth's perception of his or her chance of being successful in legitimate society, or because of an enhanced self-image as a law-abiding citizen. It is expected that youths in the restitution programs will have a greater sense of citizenship, show more remorse for their crimes, and have an increased sense that their disposition was fair.

4
Juvenile Offenders: Methods and Measures

Introduction

Social science research often suffers from serious methodological problems, including limited scope and generalizability of the studies, weak or inadequate research designs from which to make causal inferences, and unreliable measurement of key concepts. Findings from one jurisdiction, even if a sufficient level of internal validity has been established, are not generalizable to another jurisdiction and replication of studies using similar concepts and measures is rare. Although sophisticated statistical techniques are available to deal with nonequivalent comparison group designs, the problems introduced by selective assignment of persons to different programs are immense. Statistical controls may not adjust sufficiently to permit reliable conclusions. Finally, unreliable measurement of key concepts has a devastating effect on statistical analysis. Unreliable measurement of the dependent variable (recidivism, in this study) seriously depresses the amount of variance that can be explained, because error cannot be explained by independent variables. Thus, relationships usually are underestimated and tests of significance are likely to reveal no difference even when one actually exists.

In the post-positivist era, it has become common to recognize that most theories of decisions and behavior are contingent, and that the circumstances under which propositions are tested must be quite similar if similar results are to be expected. Findings also may be sensitive to the particular measurement used and to the type of analysis undertaken. Multiplism (Cook, 1985) is one approach for avoiding some of the problems that too often have plagued research. Multiplism involves using multiple methods, multiple sites, multiple measures, and so forth in an effort to examine the stability of findings across different contexts and analysis styles.

Insofar as possible, a multiplism approach has been used in this research. Propositions will be tested in each of the six sites, whenever possible, in an effort to determine the stability of findings across the different contexts found in the six cities. Whenever possible, multiple measures of key concepts will be tested and compared, to insure that the results are not overly sensitive to the particular measurement used. Finally, the design that underlies the study of perceptions and recidivism is, by necessity, quasi-experimental: it is impossible to randomly assign persons to various perceptions of certainty, severity, and so forth. For this part of the study, multiple regression analysis for all cases pooled and for each site will be used to examine the stability of alternative models linking perceptions to recidivism. In the second part of the analysis, examining the effect of experiences in the juvenile justice system on perceptions and subsequent crimes, juveniles were randomly assigned to restitution dispositions or to traditional dispositions, including probation and incarceration. Field experiments, however, never approach the purity of the laboratory, and there were numerous problems in implementing and maintaining the integrity of the experiments. Nevertheless, the resulting designs certainly are stronger and more powerful than those normally produced by the highly selective decision processes common in the juvenile justice system.

Sources of Data

Data for the study were obtained from in-person interviews and official court records of 876 adjudicated delinquents in six juvenile courts: Washington, D.C.; Ventura, California; Dane County (Madison), Wisconsin; Oklahoma County (Oklahoma City), Oklahoma; Clayton County (Jonesboro), Georgia; and Ada County (Boise), Idaho. These data were collected in conjuction with the national evaluation of the juvenile restitution programs funded by the National Institute of Juvenile Justice and Delinquency Prevention. Six sites were selected out of the 85 sites included in the federal program for an intensive evaluation that included experimental designs to compare the effect of restitution, probation, and incarceration on recidivism, victim attitudes, and other aspects of the juvenile justice system. Because the primary emphasis in the study was the comparison of restitution with traditional dispositions, the sites were selected on the basis of diversity in the types of restitution programs and the comparisons that could be made, the geographical diversity, and the overall management capacity of the juvenile system.

Characteristics of the Interviewed Sample

All juveniles included in this study had been convicted of offenses that would have been crimes if committed by adults and many would be considered in the categories of serious and chronic offenders (see Table 4.1).

The average age was almost 16 years, and more than 65 percent were 16 or over when they entered the program. Eighty-seven percent of the juveniles were males. Sixty-one percent had one or more prior offenses

TABLE 4.1. Characteristics of the Interviewed Sample.

	All Sites	Ventura CA	Washington D.C.	Clayton County GA	Boise ID	Oklahoma County OK	Dane County WI
# Cases	857	112	168	176	105	101	195
AGE							
Average	15.8	16.0	16.1	15.3	15.4	15.5	16.2
12 & Under	2 %	1 %	2 %	6 %	2 %	3 %	0 %
13	4	4	2	3	12	11	0
14	10	7	9	15	12	12	4
15	19	17	13	22	20	16	21
16	29	30	27	30	26	30	32
17	26	28	29	24	21	21	28
18	10	13	16	0	6	7	14
19	0	1	1	0	0	0	0
GENDER							
% Male	87	95	82	81	87	85	
OFFENSES							
% With 1 or More Priors	61	71	63	55	71	64	53
% With 1 or More Subsequents	60	80	58	57	60	55	53
TYPE OF OFFENSE							
% Robbery, Rape Aggrevated Assault	7	2	27	1	0	8	3
% Burglary	31	54	25	22	30	30	33
% Larceny	36	21	36	50	39	47	34
% Non-Aggr. Assault	3	0	5	4	2	1	3
% Forgery, Embezzl.	3	9	1	1	5	2	4
% Other Minor	16	10	4	20	23	10	23
% Trivial & Status	2	5	1	2	2	3	1

TABLE 4.1. (*cont.*)

	All sites	Ventura CA	Washington D.C.	Clayton County GA	Boise ID	Oklahoma County OK	Dane County WI
ETHNICITY							
% White	70	78	1	95	99	58	96
% Black	26	4	99	4	0	34	4
% Mexican	18						
% Am. Indian						8	
% Asian	1			1			
% Other/Mixed					1		
SCHOOL							
% In School	67	64	49	66	79	76	75
Reason for Not Being in School							
% Dropped out	56	57	40	60	47	65	63
% Expelled	20	14	30	10	47	17	17
% Suspended	2	3	5	2	0	4	0
% Incarcerated	3	0	5	6	0	4	0
% Temporarily Out	4	3	5	6	0	0	4
% Home Study	.5			1			
% Working	5	6	5	8	0	4	4
% Graduated	9	17	10	4	6	4	11

FAMILY							
% Lives with Neither Parent	9	9	6	4	6	8	18
% Lives with Mother	33	26	53	28	27	44	22
% Lives with Father	4	5	4	4	5	1	5
% Lives with Both	53	59	36	62	59	46	54
Average Years in School							
Mother	11.7	11.5	12	11	12.2	11.4	12.4
Father	12.1	12.2	11.7	11.3	13.3	11.5	12.7
JOBS							
1 Previous Job	72	40	83	87	91	66	60
2 Previous Jobs	25	57	15	13	9	32	33
3 Previous Jobs	33	3	2	0	0	2	7
4 Previous Jobs	.2						
% Currently Emp.	36	48	28	41	38	43	48
% Looking for Work	54	56	77	46	46	52	49

and 60 percent were rereferred to juvenile or adult court for crimes during the three-year period after entering the programs from which these data were drawn. The juveniles averaged 1.7 prior contacts with the juvenile court during the two years before entry to the program and 1.3 subsequent contacts in the 2.5 years of followup.

The types of offenses committed by these juveniles also lean toward the more serious side. Seven percent were convicted of robbery, rape, or aggravated assault and 31 percent for burglary. An additional 36 percent were convicted of larceny, which qualifies as a Part I index offense in the uniform crime reporting (UCR) index. Only two percent entered the program as the result of a status offense or other victimless crime, such as possession of alcohol or drugs.

In Washington, D.C., almost all the juveniles were black, whereas white youths dominated in the other sites. Ventura had a sizable group of Mexicans (18 percent) and Oklahoma county had 8 percent who were American Indian.

Sixty-seven percent of the juveniles were in school, but in Washington, D.C., only 49 percent were enrolled in school. Of those who were not in school, most had dropped out (56 percent) or been suspended or expelled (22 percent). Although 90 percent of the juveniles said they had been employed previously, only 72 percent could actually name a specific employer. Twenty-eight percent had held more than one job.

The family situations for the youngsters in the study were similar to those expected among a group of juvenile offenders: 37 percent were in one-parent families, 9 percent lived with neither parent, and 53 percent lived with two parents. In Washington, D.C., only 36 percent of the juvenile delinquents lived with two parents. Sixty-eight percent of the mothers had jobs, according to the juveniles, and 90 percent of the fathers were employed at the time of the surveys. Average years of schooling for the mothers was 11.7 years compared with 12.1 for the fathers.

Although the sample is not necessarily representative of all juvenile delinquents as it overrepresents the more chronic and serious cases, it is an appropriate sample for a policy-oriented study of perceptions and illegal behavior. Juveniles similar to those included in this study commit most of the juvenile crime and it is at this group that crime control policies are directed. Thus, it is especially appropriate to conduct a study linking policy responses, perceptions, and recidivism for this group of youngsters.

The Juvenile Offender Interviews

The interviews with the juvenile offenders were conducted in person by a trained member of the research team at the end of the court's jurisdiction over the youth or at the end of one year beyond disposition, whichever occurred first. The 876 interviews that were obtained represented a

63 percent completion rate. The interviewers met with the youth in his or her home or at a neutral location. No other persons were present at the time of the interview. The interview schedule is shown in Appendix A. All of the attitude variables and other information about the youths' job history and parents were based on data from the interviews.

The Official Records Check

Data on prior and subsequent offenses were obtained from an official records check that was conducted approximately two years after the last of the cases included in the study had exited from the programs. Because most of the youths spent about a year in the programs, the full followup period was almost three years from time of entry. For convenience, all offenses that occurred after entry to the program are called subsequent offenses, even though for much of the analysis these will be divided into "in-program" reoffenses and "post-program" reoffenses.

All offense data were obtained from a search of official court records of referrals to juvenile or adult court in the county where the youth was adjudicated. This search was undertaken by a coding team from the Institute of Policy Analysis, under the direction of the national evaluators.

The data collected from the official records included, for each offense, the type of offense, date, how the case was processed (e.g., informal adjustment, formal, waiver to adult court, dismissed for lack of evidence), and the sanctions. Up to three sanctions could be coded for each offense. If the youth was detained or incarcerated in conjunction with the offense, the dates entering and leaving the facility were recorded, for up to three separate entries and departures per offense. There were no limitation on the number of priors and subsequents, and all that were found in the file during the relevant time periods were coded.

The type of offense was classified according to local crime codes and converted to a common coding system for the six jurisdictions. For the most part, these codes conform to the Uniform Crime Report categories for Part I offenses and to the UCR definitions for Part II offenses. The number of offenses was based on the number of discrete criminal events, occurring at different places and at different points in time, not the number of charges arising from the events. Thus, a burglary would count only as one offense, even though the youth might also have been charged with trespassing or possession of stolen property as a result of the same episode. Theft of several items from a household would count only as one offense. A crime spree, however, that yielded five cases of vandalism involving separate places over a period of several hours or days, would count as five separate offenses.

The analysis includes cases handled informally, but any subsequent offenses that were eventually dismissed for lack of evidence or for which the person was exonerated were excluded from the analysis.

Coding reliability was maintained by having the data collectors verify the coding on 10 percent of the files. Also, since the coders worked as a team, in the same location, specific coding conventions were developed to deal with problems unique to the jurisdiction. Because the same coders collected the data from all six sites, a considerable degree of uniformity was achieved in the coding of data.

The subsequent risk time was defined as the time lag between date of entry to the program through the date the records were searched in each jurisdiction. The records search for prior offenses extended to two years before the date of entry to the program for each case.

Management Information System Data

The final source of data for the study is the management information system established by the national evaluators for all six experimental sites, as well as for 79 other courts with restitution programs that were part of the implementation study. The management information system included an intake and closure form for each case. These were completed by program personnel and forwarded to the national evaluators in Eugene, Oregon, each week for analysis. In the experimental sites, intake and control forms were completed on all cases in the control group, as well as on those in the experimental groups. A research assistant, employed by the national evaluation team, worked with each of the six experimental programs and was responsible for completing these forms, as well as for conducting the interviews with the juveniles and maintaining the integrity of the random assignment.

The management information system data included the age, race, and sex of the youth; the evaluation group to which he or she was assigned; the actual disposition of the case by the court (including "crossover" assignments); the details of the restitution plan and other dispositions, such as the number of days detained or incarcerated; and information on whether the case was closed successfully.

Offenders and Offense Rates

Measures of Offense Rates

Many different recidivism variables were created from the official records and examined for suitability. These are: (see Figure 4.1 for a quick summary):

1. ANYSUB. Those who had any subsequent offenses on record were scored "1," others "0." This is a measure of the prevalence or "participation" in criminal activity.

FIGURE 4.1. Summary of Offense Indicators

ANYSUB....	0 = none; 1 = one or more
SUB...........	Number of subsequents during risk period
SUB1..........	Annual rate of subsequents (SUB ÷ risk time)
SSER..........	Seriousness index
SSER1........	Annual seriousness index (SSER ÷ risk time)
SFEL.........	Number of felonies
SFEL1........	Annual rate of falonies (SFEL ÷ risk time)
Lambda.......	Estimated annual offense rate for those with at least one subsequent offense (Lambda1 is estimated from the time between the first two offenses; Lambda2 from the time between the second and third offenses, etc.)
SUB11........	Annual rate, excluding from risk time the days incarcerated
SSER11.......	Annual seriousness rate, excluding from risk time the days incarcerated
LSUB.........	Natural log, number of subsequents
LSUB1.......	Natural log, annual offense rate
LSSER.......	Natural log, seriousness index
LSSER1......	Natural log, annual seriousness index
LSFEL.......	Natural log, number of felonies
LSFEL1......	Natural log, annual felony rate
PRIOR........	Number of priors, two years before entry
PSER..........	Prior seriousness index
LPRIOR......	Natural log, number of priors
LPSER.......	Natural log, prior seriousness index

2. SUB. SUB is the total number of subsequents for each person during the risk period.
3. SUB1. Because the time at risk differed among individuals, the measure of subsequents was converted to an annual rate of reoffending by dividing the number of subsequents by the number of days at risk: SUB1 = subsequents/risk time. This is an annual incident rate.
4. SUB2. Persons who had not committed any subsequent offenses were at risk for varying lengths of time, some as little as 18 months, others for almost four years. The offense rate SUB1 does not take into account the differing risk periods for nonrecidivist and all nonrecidivist will have a score of zero (0/risk time = 0). To rectify this problem, SUB2 was created by adding a small constant (0.01) to the numerator and then dividing by time at risk. Thus, SUB2 = (subsequents + 0.01)/risk time. This permits persons who were crime-free for a longer period of time to have better scores than those who were crime-free for a shorter period of time. As it turned out, this correction factor was not needed in the data, as the correlation between SUB2 and SUB1 was 1.0. There were no persons who remained crime-free for 18 months and then committed another offense. Thus, this variable is not considered further in the analysis.

In addition to these measures of recidivism, another set was created to reflect differing levels of crime seriousness. The weights used in determining crime seriousness are somewhat arbitrary, but they are based on the Sellin-Wolfgang seriousness scale (Sellin & Wolfgang, 1969). This scale, however, produces a badly skewed variable if certain crimes (rape and aggravated assault, for example) are given the excessively high scores reflecting public views of their relative seriousness. To improve the property of the variable, a simple weighting system was created that permits differentiation among different levels of seriousness, but does not produce outliers in the data that later will confound the analysis. The weighting system is shown in Figure 4.2.

5. SSER. This measure of recidivsm weights each subsequent by its seriousness (SSER = (SUB01 * WT01) + SUB02* WT02) . . . + (SUBn * WTn).
6. SSER1. The weighted seriousness scale, SSER, is corrected to an annualized rate by dividing by risk time to produce SSER1.
7. SFEL The number of felonies committed by the juveniles is used as an alternative to the other measures of seriousness. Because the definition of "felony" differs from one state to another, a common definition was provided: rape, robbery (armed or unarmed), aggravated assault (i.e., assault with a dangerous weapon or with injury requiring medical attention), burglary, arson of buildings or residences, and theft involving losses of $50 or more.
8. SFEL1. By dividing the number of felonies by the risk time, an annual felony rate is constructed.
10. SUB11. This variable is created by dividing the number of subsequent offenses (SUB) by the time at risk after subtracting the number of days incarcerated during the risk period. (SUB11 = subsequents/(risk time-number of days incarcerated). There are problems with this variable, however, because offenses were committed by the juveniles during the time they presumably were incarcerated. These offenses were not removed from the data, since they are actual offenses committed against other residents or staff, or against outsiders during periods of leave from the institution, or AWOL (absent without leave).
11. SSER11. This correction removes incarceration days from the time at risk for the seriousness measure, SSER1.

FIGURE 4.2. Weighting System for Measures of Crime Seriousness

Type of crime	Weight
1. Rape, armed robbery, aggravated assault	5
2. Burglary, attempted burglary, arson	4
3. Motor vehicle theft, forgery, fraud, embezzlement, and other felony property offenses	3
4. Simple assault, resisting an officer, fights, other personal incidents, and minor property offenses such as receiving stolen property, vandalism, disorderly conduct, shoplifting, theft, and purse snatching	2
5. Trivial victimless crimes including drug possession, trespassing, and violations of city ordinances (curfew)	1

12. LAMBDA1 . . . LAMBDA5. Lambda is an estimated rate of reoffending for those who reoffended at all (Blumstein et al., 1978). Lambda is found by calculating the number of days between subsequent offenses, and converting to an estimated annual rate. Thus, LAMBDA1 is found by dividing the number of days between the first and second subsequents into 365 days. Lambda2 is the annualized rate between the second and third offenses, and so on up to five reoffenses. Five different versions of Lambda were created for comparison purposes and to estimate the stability of this measure of offending.
13. LSUB, LSUB1, LSSER, LSSER1. Many of the recidivism variables produced through the procedures described earlier were badly skewed, thereby reducing or distorting their relationship to other variables. Thus, another set of variables was produced by taking the natural log of SUB, SUB1, SSER, and SSER1. (A constant of 1.0 wts added to each variable before taking its log). These variables are designated as LSUB, LSUB1, and so forth.
14. ANYPRIOR, PRIOR, PSER. These different measures of priors were created in a manner parallel to the indicators of subsequents. The first, ANYPRIOR, is a dichotomous variable with zero indicating no priors and one indicating one or more priors. PRIOR, is the number of prior offenses during the two-year time period before the youth committed the offense that resulted in referral to the program. A seriousness measure of priors, PSER, was obtained using the same weighted scale as used in the analysis of subsequents. Because the risk period for priors was two years for all cases, there was no need to divide by time at risk.
15. LPRIOR, LPSER. These variables are the natural log of the variables defined earlier, PRIOR and PSER.

Risk time was computed as the difference between the date of referral to the program, or the date of exit from the program, and the date the records search was conducted in each location.

Comparing Alternative Measures of Recidivism

How much difference does the operationalization of recidivism make in the analysis? Recent controversies about the measure of recidivism find some scholars arguing that distinctions must be made betweeen participation (the percentage who commit any subsequent offense) and frequency (the time-specific offense rate for those who commit at least one subsequent offense), and that failure to take this into account has obscured the true relationship between predictor variables and criminality (Blumstein, Cohen, & Farrington, 1988). Others (Gottfredson & Hirschi, 1988) disagree:

> Contrary to Blumstein et al.'s predictions, and to the general thrust of the career model . . . the researcher could focus on incidence, participation, or even on

lambda in its various definitions without concern. We grant variation in the correlation coefficients. . . . We assert only that the direction, pattern, and relative magnitude of the correlations are much the same for all measures.

Table 4.2 shows the correlations among all of the different measures of recidivism. Several points should be made.

First, the measure of participation (ANYSUB) is related to the measures of offense rate and offense seriousness, but the correlations are not particularly strong, averaging less than .50 between ANYSUB and SUB (the number of subsequents), SUB1 (annual rate of subsequents), SSER (seriousness index), SSER1 (annual seriousness rate), SFEL (number of felonies), and SFEL1 (the annual felony rate). However, the size of these correlations appears to be reduced considerably due to the skewness of the various measures of subsequent rates. When the natural logarithm of the frequency and seriousness measures are used, the correlations with ANYSUB are considerably higher, averaging .68. ANYSUB cannot be correlated with Lambda, of course, because only the cases with at least one subsequent were used in the calculation of Lambda.

Second, the measures of frequency and measures of seriousness are rather closely related. For example, SUB (the number of subsequents) is

TABLE 4.2a. Correlation Matrix of Recidivism Variables.

	ANY	SUB	SUB1	SSER	SSER1	SFEL	SFEL1
ANYSUB	1.00						
SUB	.53	1.00					
SUB1	.54	.97	1.00				
SSER	.51	.94	.92	1.00			
SSER1	.50	.90	.94	.97	1.00		
SFEL	.35	.64	.67	.84	.86	1.00	
SFEL1	.32	.60	.67	.78	.85	.97	1.00
AVG	.45	.76	.85	.82	.83	.72	.69
LAMBDA1		.29	.32	.26	.28	.16	.16
LAMBDA2		.20	.22	.21	.21	.15	.15
LAMBDA3		.15	.17	.13	.15	.10	.10
LAMBDA4		.02	.02	.02	.02	.03	.03
LAMBDA5		.22	.27	.18	.23	.09	.09
SUB11	.47	.88	.91	.86	.87	.03	.63
SSER11	.43	.79	.83	.86	.89	.76	.75
LSUB	.82	.87	.87	.83	.81	.59	.53
LSUB1	.74	.91	.93	.87	.88	.62	.59
LSSER	.83	.81	.81	.84	.82	.66	.60
LSSER1	.76	.84	.87	.88	.89	.71	.67
LSFEL	.48	.63	.64	.83	.81	.90	.83
LSFEL1	.44	.63	.67	.83	.86	.94	.91
AVG (1)	.68	.78	.80	.85	.85	.74	.69

1. The averages shown at the bottom of the table are average correlations between the variable along the top and the logged values shown in the last six rows of the table.

TABLE 4.2b. Correlation Matrix of Recidivism Variables.

	LD1	LD2	LD3	LD4	LD5	SUB11	SSER11	LSUB	LSUB1	LSS	LSS1	LSFEL
LD1	1.00											
LD2	.06	1.00										
LD3	.09	.01	1.00									
LD5	.19	−.06	.01	1.00								
LD6	−.05	.00	.14	.14	1.00							
SUB11	.29	.16	.15	.03	.24	1.00						
SSER11	.15	.14	.12	.00	.18	.95	1.00					
LSUB	.36	.23	.16	.04	.24	.77	.70	1.00				
LSUB1	.39	.25	.19	.03	.31	.83	.76	.98	1.00			
LSSER	.33	.26	.14	.05	.18	.72	.70	.97	.94	1.00		
LSSER1	.35	.28	.16	.04	.26	.78	.77	.95	.96	.98	1.00	
LSFEL	.20	.18	.09	.06	.09	.61	.72	.67	.68	.78	.71	1.00
LSFEL1	.20	.18	.10	.06	.09	.65	.77	.65	.68	.75	.67	.98
AVG (1)								.84	.84	.88	.85	.76

1. The averages shown at the bottom of the table are average correlations between the variable along the top and the logged values shown in the last six rows of the table.

correlated with SSER (the seriousness index) at .94 and with the number of felonies (SFEL) at .64. SSER is correlated with SFEL at .84.

Third, the correction for risk time did not make much difference, as SUB is correlated with SUB1 at .97; and SSER is correlated with SSER1 at .97. This almost certainly is due to the relatively long risk time for all cases—a minimum of 18 months.

Fourth, the correction used in SUB11 and SSER11, in which days incarcerated were removed from risk time, made some difference, but not a great deal. SUB1 correlates with SUB11 at .91; and SSER1 correlates with SSER11 at .89.

Fifth, the logged values perform better than the regular (skewed) values. For example, the average intercorrelation of SUB with the other measures of frequency, prevalence, and seriousness is .78; the average intercorrelation of LSUB with these other variables is .84. On the whole, the intercorrelations of the logged variables exceed those of the regular variables by amounts ranging from .02 to .08.

Finally, the measures of Lambda do not correlate as highly with one another or with any of the other measures of subsequent offenses. This is partly due to the fact that the cases upon which these correlations are based differ from the others since all cases with no subsequents have missing values on Lambda. Similarly, the low intercorrelations among the Lambda variables themselves could be due to the gradually diminishing number of cases. The reader should recall that Lambda1 is an annual rate estimated by calculating the time between the immediate offense and the first subsequent; Lambda2 is an annual rate estimated by calculating the time between the first subsequent and the second, and so forth.

To determine whether the low correlations are due to instability in the estimates or to the changing population upon which the correlations are based, another analysis was done of the 241 cases that had at least three subsequent offenses. These results are shown in Table 4.3, and indicate that Lambda—when estimated from only two offense points—is very unstable, with an average interitem correlation of only .05. Further, the correlations with other measures of subsequents remain quite low, with only one exceeeding .30. It is important to point out here that all cases in the 241-case analysis have at least three subsequent offenses. Thus, SUB, SUB1, and the logged values of these variables are measures of the rate of offending among those who reoffend, just as Lambda is a measure of the rate of reoffending among those who reoffend. The SUB variables are based on more data—namely, the total number of offenses during the risk period, corrected for time at risk; whereas Lambda is based on only two pieces of information, the time between one offense and the next. Thus, the SUB variables should be a more accurate indicator of offense rates for persons who reoffend; the low correlations with Lambda are a clear indication that offense rates based on annual projections from time between two offenses contain considerable error variance.

TABLE 4.3. Operationalizing "Lambda": Alternative Variables.

N=241	Lambda1	Lambda2	Lambda3
Lambda1	1.00	.05	.09
Lambda2	.05	1.00	.01
Lambda3	.09	.01	1.00
SUB	.21	.18	.15
SUB 1	.26	.20	.17
SSER	.14	.17	.13
SSER1	.19	.18	.15
LSUB	.26	.21	.16
LSUB1	.33	.24	.19
LSSER	.15	.22	.14
LSSER1	.22	.24	.16

Figures are the zero order correlations among the alternative measure of offense rates for the 241 persons who had committed at least three subsequent offenses.

Definitions:

Lambda1 – annual rate estimated from time lag between offense 0 and 1

Lambda2 – annual rate estimated from time lag between offense 1 and 2

Lambda3 – annual rate estiamted from time lag between offense 2 and 3

SUB – # of subsequents

SUB1 – SUB/risktime

SSER – seriousness index

SSER1 – seriousness index, corrected for time at risk

LSUB..LSSER1 – natural logarithim of SUB, SUB1, etc.

Another technique for choosing among multiple measures of a particular concept is to examine the stability of correlations with commonly used predictor variables. The results are shown in Table 4.4. The conclusions are virtually the same as reached when examining the interitem correlations. The measures of frequency (SUB, SUB1) and the measures of seriousness correlate in about the same way with the predictor variables, school, female, living with both parents, and age. The variable representing minorities, however, correlates considerably better with the measures of seriousness, indicating that minority youth are not more likely to be rereferred to court, but that they are referred for more serious offenses. The logged variables generally perform better than the nonlogged values, with an increase in the correlation coefficient of .01 or .02. The correction for days incarcerated did not influence the correlations at all. Finally, the Lambda estimates do not correlate in the same manner as the other measures with any of the predictor variables. In many instances, the di-

TABLE 4.4. Demographics and Alternative Measures of Subsequents.

	Not in School	Minority	Female	Both Parents	Age
ANYSUB	.10*	.02	−.12*	−.03	−.05
SUB (# Subs)	.11*	.02	−.09*	−.05	−.08*
SUB1 (Yr. Rate)	.10*	.03	−.08*	−.05	−.09*
SSER (Serious)	.11*	.09*	−.11	−.08*	−.08*
SSER1 (Ser. Rate)	.11*	.09*	−.10	−.07*	−.08*
SFEL (# Felonies)	.08*	.11*	−.08	−.09*	−.05
SFEL1 (Fel Rate)	.08*	.10*	−.05	−.08*	−.04
Lambda1 (N=511)	.06	−.07*	−.01	−.02	.06
Lambda2 (N=342)	−.06	00	−.01	−.08	−.17*
Lambda3 (N=241)	−.05	−.04	−.02	−.07	.02
Lambda4 (N=130)	−.05	.10	.00	.05	−.08
Lambda5 (N=74)	.07	.05	.01	.00	.05
SUB11 (incarceration correction)	.12*	.05	−.08*	−.04	−.08*
SSER11 (incarceration correction)	.12*	.10*	−.09*	−.06	−.07*
LSUB (Ln SUB)	.13*	.04	−.13*	−.05	−.09*
LSUB1 (Ln SUB1)	.12*	.05	−.12*	−.05	−.10*
LSSER (Ln SSER)	.13*	.10*	−.15*	−.07*	−.09*
LSSER1 (Ln SSER1)	.12*	.12*	−.15*	−.07*	−.10*
LSFEL (Ln SFEL)	.10*	.17*	−.14*	−.09*	−.07*
LSfel1 (Ln SFEL1)	.09*	.15*	−.12*	−.08*	−.07*

Figures are the zero order correlation coefficients. An asterisk * indicates statistical significance beyond .05, one-tailed test. N=857 except for the offense rates, Lambda, which are calculated only for persons who have subsequent offenses.

rection of the relationship is opposite that of the other measures of recidivism. Furthermore, whereas almost all the relationships using the standard measures of recidivism are statistically significant, only two of the correlations with Lambda are significant (at .05), and one of these is in the wrong direction.

Table 4.5 shows the correlations between the multiple indicators of recidivism and several of the major independent variables used in the study. The results are essentially identical to those discussed previously. Variables that show statistically significant relationships with any of the measures (excepting the Lambda estimates), show significant relationships with the other indicators. Those that are marginally significant (such as certainty of punishment) show stable marginally significant relationships. It should be noted that the direction of the relationships between recidivism and the three deterrence variables are in the wrong direction: those who believe their punishment will be more certain and severe were more likely to commit subsequent offenses and they committed more serious offenses. Similarly with celerity: a longer time lag between the offense and disposition was correlated with lower recidivism rates.

It is apparent that several different indicators of recidivism would serve equally well in the analysis. As an overall indicator of subsequent of-

TABLE 4.5. Deterrence Variables and Alternative Measures of Subsequents.

N=857	INTENT	SERIOUS	SCORE	CERTAIN	CELERITY	RESTN (random)	RESTN (actual)
ANYSUB	.10*	.06*	.07*	.01	−.12*	−.07*	−.08*
SUB (# Subs)	.12*	.06*	.10*	.06*	−.10*	−.08*	−.08*
SUB1 (Yr. Rate)	.11*	.05	.11*	.07*	−.11*	−.07*	−.08*
SSER (Serious)	.11*	.06*	.11*	.03	−.08*	−.07*	−.08*
SSER1 (Ser. Rate)	.10*	.05	.12*	.05	−.09*	−.06*	−.08*
SFEL (# Felonies)	.07*	.03	.09*	00	−.05	−.03	−.05
SFEL1 (Fel Rate)	.06*	.03	.08*	.02	−.06	−.03	−.05
Lambda1	.05	.01	.10*	.03	−.26*	.04	.06
Lambda2	−.03	−.09	.07	.06	.02	.05	.04
Lambda3	.02	00	.01	−.05	−.09	−.12*	−.12*
Lambda4	00	−.03	.04	.02	.05	.07	.07
Lambda5	.10	.07	−.09*	.05	.04	−.03	−.07
SUB11 (-Incar)	.10*	.07*	.09*	.05*	−.11*	−.07*	−.08*
SSER11 (-Inca)	.08*	.07*	.10*	.03	−.10*	−.06*	−.07*
LSUB (Ln SUB)	.13*	.07*	.11*	.04	−.13*	−.07*	−.08*
LSUB1 (Ln SUB)	.13*	.06*	.12*	.06*	−.13*	−.07*	−.09*
LSSER (Ln SSER)	.14*	.07*	.12*	.02	−.12*	−.07*	−.09*
LSSER1 (Ln SSER1)	.13*	.06*	.14*	.04	−.12*	−.07*	−.10*
LSFEL (Ln SFEL)	.12*	.04	.10*	−.00	−.06*	−.06*	−.09*
LSfe11 (Ln SFEL1)	.10*	.04	.10*	.01	−.07*	−.05*	−.08*

Figures are the zero order correlation coefficients. An asterisk indicates statistical significance beyond .05, one-tailed test. Variables along the top are INTENT (intentions to commit subsequent crimes); SERIOUS (seriousness of the immediate offense); CERTAIN (likelihood of punishment); CELERITY (days between offense and disposition, high numbers mean longer delays); RESTN (random) persons randomly assigned to restitution or to a control condition; RESTN (actual) persons actually in restitution programs or control conditions, where: RESTN = 1; traditional dispositions =0.

fenses, the best two indicators probably are LSUB1 (the natural logarithm of the number of subsequent offenses, divided by time at risk), and LSSER1, the natural logarithm of the seriousness index, divided by time at risk. Thus, these two indicators of subsequents will be used in most of the analysis. If the results are essentially the same, only LSUB1 will be reported.

Measuring Prior Offenses

Table 4.6 shows the intercorrelations among the five possible measures of prior offenses, and Table 4.7 shows how these correlate with the different measures of subsequents. ANYPRIOR, the dichotomous measure that divides first offenders from all others, correlates at 0.53 and 0.56, respectively, with PRIOR (the number of prior offenses) and PSER (the seriousness index), but the correlations increase substantially (to 0.82 and 0.86) with the logged values of these variables. The logged values of PRIOR and PSER correlate with one another at 0.97.

As expected, the correlations with subsequents follow the same patterns observed previously. The logged values of prior offenses have the best fit with the logged values of subsequent offenses. Thus, the variable that will be used in the analysis will be LPRIOR.

Perceptions and Values

Intentions

Intentions to commit subsequent crimes and certainty of being caught were both assessed using a 100-point likelihood scale. Near the end of the 35-minute interview, the juvenile was given a card with a zero- to 100-point likelihood scale on it (see Figure 4.3) and asked a series of simple questions about future events, such as the likelihood that he or she would go to a movie within the next week. After the youngster understood the

TABLE 4.6. Alternative Measures of Prior Offenses.

	ANYPRIOR	PRIOR	LPRIOR	PSER	LPSER
ANYPRIOR	1.00				
PRIOR	.56	1.00			
LnPRIOR	.82	.90	1.00		
PSER (Seriousness)	.53	.94	.84	1.00	
LnPSER	.86	.83	.97	.83	1.00

Figures are the zero order correlation coefficients. ANYPRIOR is a dummy-coded variable with 0 for no priors, 1 for any prior; PRIOR is the number of priors during the two-year time period before the immediate offense; LPRIOR is the natural logarithim of PRIOR; PSER is the additive seriousness index for priors; and LPSER is the natural log of PSER.

TABLE 4.7. Intercorrelation of Alternative Measures of Priors and Subsequents.

	ANY PRIOR	PRIOR	LPRIOR	PSER	LPSER
ANYSUB	.22	.22	.25	.18	.25
SUB (# Subs)	.22	.26	.28	.22	.27
SUB1 (Yr. Rate)	.24	.24	.28	.21	.27
SSER (Serious)	.22	.20	.24	.19	.25
SSER1 (Ser. Rate)	.23	.20	.24	.19	.25
SFEL (# Felonies)	.18	.10	.15	.11	.14
SFEL1 (Fel Rate)	.17	.08	.14	.09	.13
Lambda1	.24	.18	.24	.13	.23
Lambda2	.12	.02	.06	00	.05
Lambda3	.11	.06	.01	.08	.03
Lambda4	.04	.02	00	.01	00
Lambda5	.17	.05	.09	.02	.08
SUB11 (−Inclar)	.21	.22	.26	.19	.25
SSER11 (−Incar)	.19	.16	.21	.15	.20
LSUB (Ln SUB)	.27	.27	.32	.23	.32
LSUB1 (Ln SUB1)	.27	.27	.32	.23	.32
LSSER (Ln SSER)	.28	.25	.30	.22	.30
LSSER1 (Ln SSER1)	.28	.24	.30	.22	.31
LSFEL (Ln SFEL)	.22	.14	.20	.13	.19
LSfe11 (Ln SFEL1)	.17	.12	.19	.13	.17

Figures are the zero order correlation coefficients. Generally, coefficients greater than .02 were statistically significant at .05 or greater.

scale, the interviewer then asked a question about intentions to commit subsequent offenses:

Before asking the next question, I would like to remind you that you do not have to answer questions, but I hope you will. All of your answers will be kept confidential. What are the chances that you would do the same kind of thing again [BRIEF DESCRIPTION OF OFFENSE] in the next year? What number best represents the chances that you would do this again in the next year?

FIGURE 4.3. Likelihood scale.

0 10 20 30 40 50 60 70 80 90 100

|-|-|-|-|-|-|-|-|-|-|-|-|-|-|-|-|-|-|-|-|-|-|-|-|-|-|-|-|-|-|-|-|-|-|-|-|-|-|-|-|

definitely will not	probably will not	maybe	probably will	definitely will

This question was then followed with a similar one, referencing a standard offense: What are the chances that you will steal something worth $20 or more during the next year?"

These two variables were highly correlated ($r = 0.92$), but the second one was used in the analysis.

Table 4.8 shows that most of the juveniles claimed they did not intend to commit any more offenses. The mean score on the 0-to-100 likelihood scale was 14, ranging from a low of 9 in Clayton County, Georgia to a

TABLE 4.8. An Overview Of Perceptions In The Six Sites.

	All Cases N=857	Ventura 112	Washington D.C. 168	Clayton County 176	Boise 105	Oklahoma County 101	Dane County 195
Intentions							
(0 to 100 Scale)	14	17	12	9	10	12	21
Mean							
P = 0.0	51%	45%	60%	66%	56%	53%	32%
P = 1-50	45	49	37	30	43	42	58
P = 51-99	3	4	2	3	1	3	8
P = 100	1	2	1	0	0	2	1
Certainty of Referal							
(0 to 100 Scale)							
Mean	58	46	47	59	73	81	54
P = 0	11%	12%	18%	17%	3%	4%	8%
P = 1-50	38	56	49	27	26	12	47
P = 51-99	26	19	18	29	35	37	24
P = 100	25	13	15	27	36	47	22
Most Likely Sanction							
Warn & Release	1.2%	0*	3.7%	.6%	1.0%	0%	1.1
Diversion	2.6	4.0	2.5	4.2	—	1.0	2.1
Probation	8.0	1.0	11.1	12.2	0	4.0	11.7
Restitution	3.1	6.1	1.9	6.1	1.0	1.0	2.1
Prob. & Restn	3.9	2.0	1.2	2.4	1.9	1.0	9.6
Detention or Institution	80.0	84.8	79.6	71.2	96.3	92.0	69.0
Dislike Scores for Sanctions (Averages, 0 to 100 Scales)							
Warn & Release	12	14	10	13	13	14	10
Divert	44	32	42	59	55	48	31

Probation	44	40	55	47	47	48	32
Restitution	50	56	52	51	52	59	40
Detention	80	87	—	73	78	89	69
Juv Instn	92	94	93	92	95	91	93
Dislike Score for the Expected Sanction							
Score = 0	1%	1%	1%	1%	0%	1.1%	1.6%
Score = 1-50	20	20	16	21	9.5	8.5	36
Score = 51-99	39	31	30	25	71	52	37
Score = 100	40	49	54	53	19	38	25
Value Scales (1 to 7 scale)							
Good Citizen	5.0	4.5	5.4	5.1	4.6	5.6	4.7
Remorse	5.7	5.6	5.7	5.7	6.1	5.8	5.6
Fairness	5.2	5.1	5.2	5.3	5.3	5.5	4.7

For Intentions and Certainty, the first row shows the mean scores on the 0 to 100 likelihood scale; and the percentages show the proportion of respondents within specified ranges on the likelihood scale. Thus, the mean likelihood estimate for intentions to commit another crime was 14; 51% of the respondents said there was zero probability they would commit another offense; only 1% said there was a 100 percent probability.

The scale used to assess probability (likelihood) was;

Definitely Will Not	Probably Not	Maybe	Probably Will	Definitely Will

0 10 20 30 40 50 60 70 80 90 100

The value scales range from 1 to 7, with high scores, indicating attitudes that are expected to be associated with lower reoffense rates:

Lawbreaker		Good Citizen
No Remorse		Remorseful
Unfair	1 2 3 4 5 6 7	Fair

high of 21 in Dane County, Wisconsin. More than half of the juveniles said there was no chance at all they would steal something worth $20 or more.

Certainty

Certainty was measured by asking the youths to estimate the probability (on the zero-to-100 scale) of getting caught and referred to court if they stole something worth $20 or more. Eleven percent said there was no chance at all they would be caught and referred to court (see Table 4.8), but most acknowledged a relatively strong possibility of being caught. The average likelihood score was 0.58 on the 0-to-100 scale, ranging from low scores of 46 and 47 in Washington, D.C., and Ventura, California, to a high of 81 in Oklahoma County. About half of the juveniles estimated the chances of being caught and referred to court at less than 50/50.

Severity

Severity of the expected sanction was ascertained with a series of questions that followed those about intentions of committing crimes and certainty of being caught. The juveniles were handed a card showing all of the dispositions available in their jurisdiction and they were asked what they thought actually would happen to them if they stole something worth $20 or more and were caught for it. They were then asked which of the dispositions on the card they disliked the most. The interviewers led the youth through the different sanctions until all had been ranked from most disliked to least disliked. Then the juveniles were asked to actually rate their level of dislike, using a zero-to-100 "dislike" scale that was displayed on a card handed to them. With this technique, interviewers were able to determine whether the youths understood the questions. If there were discrepencies between the rankings and the scale scores, the interviewers were expected to go back over the instructions again in an effort to eliminate inaccuracies produced by confusion over the questions.

Table 4.8 shows that most of the juveniles expected to receive severe punishment, if caught. Only 1.2 percent expected to be warned and released and only 8 percent expected to be put on probation. More than 80 percent of the juveniles expected to be detained, jailed, or incarcerated for a subsequent offense. The average dislike scores for each of the possible sanctions is shown in the lower portion of Table 4.8. The results here are as expected, with the less coercive sanctions, such as warn and release, receiving lower scores on the dislike scale. Warn and release, for example, received a score of 12 overall. Diversion into some type of youth program (usually a counseling or social-service program) received the same overall dislike score as probation (44), and in Clayton and Boise, it was more disliked than probation. Restitution received higher dislike (mean = 50) scores than probation or diversion in all jurisdictions except Washington, D.C., where probation was rated higher. The perceived level of severity jumped sharply between the restitution/probation sanctions and local detention, which averaged 80 overall, and juvenile institutions received the highest overall rating, with an average score of 92.

When analyzing the data, several different estimates of sanction severity were developed. These were the average severity score (XSCORE), the score given to the least severe possible sanction (warn and release) (MINSCOR), the score given to commitment to a state juvenile institution (MAXSCOR), and the score given to the sanction the youth had previously identified as the one he or she was most likely to receive (SCORE). All of these were highly intercorrlated and performed in about the same manner in the models being tested. The variable reported in the analysis, SCORE, is the dislike score given to the sanction the youth believed he or she would actually receive.

Good Citizen Self-Image

The indicator of self-image used in the analysis represents the juvenile's identification with a "good citizen" image and set of values rather than with a "lawbreaker" image and values. During the interview, juveniles were handed a card with a series of items arrayed on a seven-point semantic differential scale. Juveniles were asked to assess their image of themselves, and then to describe how they believed others viewed them—teachers, parents, and peers. The self-image items on the questionnaire were:

(a) Troublesome/cooperative.
(b) Good/bad.
(c) Breaks rules/obeys rules.
(d) Rude/polite.
(e) Helpful to others/harmful to others
(f) Cowardly/brave.
(g) Dumb/smart.
(h) Honest/dishonest.
(i) Lazy/hardworking.
(j) Tough/weak.
(k) Not wild/wild.
(l) Mean/nice.
(m) Kind/cruel.
(n) Rich/poor.

Principal components factor analysis revealed three theoretically interesting variables. The first, called "nice/rotten" underlies the variables mean/nice, cruel/kind, rude/polite, harmful/helpful, and bad/good. The second, called "strong/wimp" contains the variables brave/coward, strong/weak, hardworking/lazy, and smart/dumb. Loading on the third, which we called "good citizen/lawbreaker" were obeying rules versus rule breaking, obeying laws versus law breaking, honest versus dishonest, and cooperative versus troublesome. Additive scales were formed comprised of these variables. The items wild/not wild and rich/poor did not load on any of these factors.

Of these three variables, the one of major theoretical interest is good citizen/lawbreaker. As shown in Table 4.8, the juveniles' views of themselves were generally more toward the good citizen side of the scale than toward the lawbreaker side, with scores between 4.5 and 5.6.

Remorse

The juvenile's sense of remorse and understanding that the crime was wrong were measured from four items in a seven-point semantic differential scale in which the youths were asked to describe their feelings about the offense they had committed. As with the other semantic differential scales, the interviewer handed the youth a card showing the items arrayed at the endpoints of a seven-point scale. The youth was asked to circle the number that corresponded to his or answer, and to report this number to the interviewer. Principal components analysis revealed a dimension nicely suited to a measure of remorse. Four variables loaded on it and are used in the scale: sorry, victim did not deserve it, wrong, and my fault. The full set of items the juveniles responded to in describing their attitudes about their crime were:

(a) Sorry/glad.
(b) Would not do it again/would do it again.
(c) Victim deserved it/did not deserve it.
(d) Wrong/right.
(e) Brave/cowardly.
(f) Legal/illegal.
(g) Dangerous/safe.
(i) My fault/not my fault.
(j) Not fun/fun.
(k) Cruel/kind
(l) Nice/mean.

Scores on the remorse scale averaged 5.7, on the seven-point scale.

Fairness

The fairness of the sanctions inflicted by the court were tapped by semantic differentials anchored with the words "fair" and "unfair" referencing the court process prior to sanction and each sanction received by the youth. Overall scores (Table 4.8) show the juveniles generally viewed the court processes as more fair than unfair, with scores between 5 and 6 on the seven-point scale.

Experiences in the Juvenile Justice System

Random Assignment

Juveniles were randomly assigned into restitution programs or into traditional dispositions in all six sites, although the characteristics of the experiments differed from one site to another. In each jurisdiction, representatives from the national evaluation and the juvenile court judge or administrator determined the specific propositions to be tested in the jurisdiction, developed definitions of eligibility, procedures for determining eligibility, and procedures for randomly selecting cases into the treatment and control groups. These were negotiated agreements, and letters detailing the agreement were sent by the evaluation team to the court, requesting a response in return showing that the plan was acceptable to the court.

Personnel from the national evaluation team were on site throughout the two or three years that the experiment operated, and were responsible for monitoring the eligibility process and for the random assignment. Although quantitative eligibility criteria were eventually negotiated with each site, eligibility decisions were always somewhat subjective. Since these decisions, however, were made long before assignment into treatment and control groups, however, variance in eligibility did not confound the design. When a case was ready for random assignment, the on-site evaluator called the national evaluators in Eugene, Oregon, who determined the assignment based on birth data, a randomly drawn multiplier, and a list of numbers for each evaluation group in that site.

The assignment was made after the determination of guilt but prior to the disposition hearing. Although this is a violation of the usual rule to assign as late as possible in the process, the dynamics of juvenile court are such that we believed fewer cross-overs (misassignments) would occur if the assignment was made prior to the presentence investigation rather than after. Since the probation officers or restitution counselors knew which program the juveniles had been selected into, they developed presentence reports consistent with those dispositions. Thus, when the case was presented to the judge for disposition, the plan would appear to be a reasonable one. Judges have a legal responsibility to look after the best interests of the youth and the community in their dispositions and, for this reason, they could and sometimes did overturn the recommendation in the presentence report. Unless otherwise specified, however, the data are analyzed in accordance with the assignments, not with actual experiences. The number of cross-overs was small enough that this made no difference in the results.

Juveniles who were rereferred to the court, and who were considered eligible for the experiment, were assigned to the same program they were in the first time. This prevented the difficult problem of determining responsibility for subsequent offenses for juveniles who had experiences in both the treatment and control groups. Also, juveniles who were co-offenders and whose cases were processed together were assigned together. Although we would have preferred that each youth be assigned individually, we believed it would be more fair to assign them together. Further, this turned out to be a relatively rare situation.

Another difficult issue pertained to when the juvenile interviews would be administered. Because the restitution program could be of very short duration (e.g., two or three months), whereas probation was considerably longer, there was a problem in determining when to administer the surveys. The best solution seemed to be to administer the interviews after the restitution portion of the sanction was complete, or one year after intake, whichever occurred first. And, the interviews for the control group were to be done at the same time so that the average length of time between intake and administration of the interview would be the same between the two groups.

The number of cases in the treatment and control groups is not equal, due to the need to insure a large-enough case flow into the restitution programs to justify the grant funds being received.

Restitution and Probation

All of the restitution programs included in the study were accountability-oriented programs emphasizing that juveniles should be held accountable for their offenses through the payment of restitution or community-service work. It would be a mistake, however, to equate restitution with punishment, as repeated surveys of program officials showed that accountability was the most important goal of restitution programs (scoring above 9 on the 10-point scale), followed by rehabilitation and victim satisfaction (scoring about 7 on the scale). Punishment was not acknowledged as a goal of restitution, as punishment usually received only a score of 2 or 3 on the scale. In the programs included here, parents were not permitted to pay restitution, and the juveniles were expected to find employment or community-service work. Program personnel worked with victims to document losses, developed restitution plans with the juveniles, provided job-preparation seminars for the youths, assisted them in developing contracts for interviews, developed community-service placements or private-sector job slots, monitored payments, and closed cases.

The probation programs required the juveniles to adhere to the rules of probation, such as curfews, school attendance, and not associating with delinquent peers. Office or home visits were held at the discretion of the probation officer.

Most of the juveniles in the restitution programs were technically on probation, but their probation requirements were monitored by restitution personnel, and the usual rules of probation, including office and home visits, were replaced with the restitution requirements. Further, their probation status was usually terminated when the restitution payments were finished.

Boise, Idaho

The experiment in Boise, Idaho, was structured to provide a comparison between restitution and short-term detention. Youths randomly selected for the restitution group were required to pay monetary restitution to the victims of their crimes or, if there was no outstanding monetary loss, they were required to complete a specified number of community-service hours. Juveniles selected into the control group were sentenced to several successive weekends of detention in a local facility. All juveniles were on probation, in addition to their requirements regarding restitution or weekend detention. The eligible group included all youths referred to court for adjudication on a delinquent offense, except those who were held in detention during the pretrial period. These cases were excluded from eligibility because the juveniles had already experienced incarceration, and thus this would not permit a valid test of restitution and detention. The assignments were followed for 89 percent of the cases assigned restitution, and for 97 percent of the cases selected into detention.

Washington, D.C.

The Washington, D.C., design provided a comparison of victim-offender mediation restitution against probation for a group of serious offenders. The court initially agreed to identify two eligible groups of offenders: those who were eligible for incarceration and those eligible for probation. Out of each group, the evaluation team would randomly select some for inclusion in the restitution program. The experiment had only operated for a short time when it was apparent that the pool of incarceration "eligibles" had shrunk drastically and was too low to generate enough cases for a separate analysis of incarceration versus restitution.

Designing an experiment for a victim offender mediation program presented some special problems. Victim offender mediation requires that both the victim and the offender voluntarily agree to participate in a mediation session. Even though eligible persons were screened for their willingness to participate in mediation, their final decisions on participation were made after disposition and assignment. Mediation cannot be successful with unwilling participants, so it did not seem reasonable (or possible) to force them into the program. Thus, the external validity of the experiment required that we permit the victim offender mediation program to take only those who were willing; yet, this would produce misassignments and weaken the internal validity. About one-third of the persons in this study who were selected for victim offender mediation chose not to participate. Those who voluntarily refused mediation did not differ much from the others, and it appears that the major factor in their refusal was advice from their lawyers. The analysis was complicated by this problem, however. As with the other cross-over problems, the data were analyzed with the cases in the group to which they were assigned, although comparisons are made with analysis when they are in the group in which they actually participated.

Clayton County, Georgia

The experiment in Clayton county compared four different treatment strategies: restitution; restitution and counseling; probation; and probation and counseling.

The restitution program involved either monetary restitution or community service. The counseling program was operated by the mental health services. In most of the analysis reported here, the restitution program is contrasted with the traditional programs. Assignments were carried out relatively well in Clayton County, with seven percent deviating from the random selection.

Oklahoma County

In Oklahoma County, random assignment was made between restitution as a sole sanction, restitution and probation, and probation. The judge in Oklahoma County reserved the right to incarcerate juveniles out of each group, and as a result 9 percent of the restitution sole sanction group were committed for incarceration, 10 percent of the restitution plus probation group, and 11 percent of the control group. This type of cross-over probably does not introduce much bias into the analysis because it occurred with relative consistency across all three groups. As in the other sites, restitution involved either monetary or community-service orders.

Ventura, California

The Ventura program presented enormous problems in maintaining the integrity of the experiment. The experiment was intended to provide a contrast between residential programs with and without restitution and probation programs with and without restitution. Two separate groups of eligibles were identified: persons eligible for out-of-home placement and persons eligible for probation. From each group, cases were randomly selected for the restitution work-release center (a residential program), and a restitution program without the residential component. Cases selected into the restitution parts of the program presented no problems. The work-release program provided a nonsecure residential facility, community-service work, job training, and job placement into paying positions. The nonresidential program provided the same services, except for the residence. Dispositions of control group cases, however, were made by a large number of people throughout the county and most were required to pay restitution. Further, several of those determined to be eligible for incarceration were not incarcerated.

Numerous efforts to stop the restitution orders on the control cases were entirely unsuccessful. Thus, this experiment ended up being a comparison of programmatic restitution (combining the two groups) and ad hoc restitution, similar to the planned design in Dane County. The ad hoc restitution approach in Ventura involved orders to pay restitution, but no mechanism for implementing them. It was determined later, through an analysis of historical records, that restitution had commonly been ordered in the juvenile court, and that the collection rate was about 35 percent. The collection rate for nonprogrammatic cases continued at about 35 percent during the course of the experiment. There apparently were no penalties for failure to pay. Thus, the comparison in Ventura is between programmatic restitution and nonprogrammatic approaches in which the juveniles are left to their own devices for complying with the orders.

Dane County, Wisconsin

The Dane County experiment was planned to contrast programmatic restitution with ad hoc restitution. As described earlier, ad hoc restitution involved restitution orders, but no implementation mechanisms. Dane County had been ordering restitution in cases where the youth was believed to have the ability to pay. The cases were handled by probation officers who normally ignored the restitution requirements, leaving the juveniles on their own. A time-series analysis of cases ordered restitution before and after the experiment revealed no change in the characteristics of persons ordered to pay restitution and no change in the successful completion rates for cases handled entirely by the probation department. There was a slight increase in the size of the orders. Thus, it appears that the experiment did not alter the way that the probation officers had been dealing with restitution cases.

Juveniles assigned to the restitution program were involved in job-preparation seminars, assistance in finding jobs in the public or private sectors, subsidized employment in both the restitution and community service components of the program, and monitoring of the plans. Juveniles assigned to probation officers were required to meet the terms of probation and to meet with the officer on a regular basis.

Program Success

Successful completion of program requirements was coded by program personnel, based on guidelines provided by the national evaluators. For the restitution programs, successful completion was defined as paying 95 percent or more of the monetary restitution ordered by the court, or working 95 percent or more of the community-service hours. For probation and incarceration, successful completion was defined as not having violated probation rules regarding school attendance, curfew, participation in treatment programs, and other similar rules. Considerable care was taken to insure that juveniles who committed offenses while under the jurisdiction of the program were not declared "unsuccessful" simply because of the offense. This would build in a correlation between program success and in-program offenses that would confound the analysis. Thus, persons who committed new offenses were judged as successful or unsuccessful in terms of their compliance with other program rules, and it was possible for juveniles to be scored as successful even though they committed another offense while in the program.

5
The Perceptual Basis of Juvenile Crime

Deterrence, labeling, equity, and social integration theories all emphasize the perceptual basis of juvenile crime, but they make different predictions about which variables will be most important or which are more sensitive to public policy influences. Deterrence theory is based on the assumption that individuals are self-interested utility maximizers who respond to the net utility (i.e., the expected net gain or lose) offered by the crime opportunity. Even if crime could be reduced by increasing the expected gain from legitimate activities through treatment or rehabilitative approaches or major changes in social conditions, these approaches are viewed as too indirect and expensive by advocates of deterrence, since the same effect could be achieved by increasing the certainty, severity, or celerity of punishment.

Other theories of choice, however, suggest that decisions are governed more by heuristics—shortcuts or rules of thumb—than by estimates of net utility, particularly under conditions of uncertainty. Decision heuristic theories suggest that individuals adopt simple rules of thumb that guide behavior and that many choices are better explained by a person's values, self-image, and the circumstances or context within which the decision emerges.

Advocates of labelling do not explain the decision-making processes that link interventions to recidivism, but the theory is more consistent with a decision heuristics perspective than with one assuming strict rationality. Labeling theory rests on the assumption that punishment, or even nonpunitive interventions by the juvenile justice system, will stigmitize juveniles, damage self-esteem, increase the likelihood that the juvenile will identify with a lawbreaking self-image rather than a good citizen image, and interfere with the juvenile's ability to be successful in normal activities such as school or work. Equity theory, or accountability approaches such as restitution, also are more consistent with decision heuristics than with strict rationality. These perspectives hold that interventions should be proportionate to the harm done and the level of culpability for the actions. The purpose of the intervention is to permit the offender to rectify the harm done, thereby restoring both the victim and the offender to their rightful places in society. Some proponents of equity theory argue that there is an inherent tendency in individuals toward fairness and balance in social or political situations (Deutsch, 1985). Sanctions that are viewed as unfair, then, may help an offender rationalize subsequent offenses; sanctions that permit individuals to repay victims and community, and that are viewed as fair, should be associated with reduced inclinations to reoffend.

Interventions such as restitution and community service are expected to be associated with increased remorse for the act, enhanced self-image as a good citizen rather than a lawbreaker, and increased perceptions that the system was fair. Thus, restitution may operate through perceptions of citizenship and fairness to reduce recidivism. Because restitution and community service both involve working at paying or volunteer positions, these experiences are expected to increase the juvenile's belief that he or she can be successful in law-abiding activities, thereby increasing their bonding to society.

The focus of this chapter is on linkage between perceptions of certainty, severity, fairness, citizenship, and remorse with self-stated intentions of committing subsequent crimes and with actual recontacts with the juvenile system during the two- or three-year followup. The effect of perceptions on intentions will be tested first in order to ascertain the consistency of a juvenile's belief systems, and then perceptions and intentions will be related to actual offenses. It is expected that perceptions of certainty, severity, remorse, and fairness will have greater predictive power for intentions than for actual crimes committed, because the circumstances and decision processes leading up to the commission of a crime are very different than the context the juvenile may have in mind when responding to the survey questionnaire.

Intentions to Reoffend

Correlates of Intentions

Perceptions of certainty and severity of punishment were related in the expected manner to juveniles' self-stated intentions to steal something worth more than $20 during the next year (see Table 5.1). Those who were more certain of being caught if they committed another offense had lower scores on the intention variable ($r = -0.16$); as did those who believed they would receive a more severe sanction ($r = -0.12$). Juveniles who were more remorseful and who believed their sanctions were fair also were less likely to say they would commit another offense. All of these relationships were statistically significant beyond 0.001.

The same pattern of relationships is found in all six sites. Certainty of

TABLE 5.1. Zero Order Correlates of Intentions.

No. of Cases	All Cases 857	Ventura CA 112	Washington D.C. 168	Clayton County GA 176	Boise ID 105	Oklahoma County OK 101	Dane County WI 195
Certainty	−.16*	−.20*	.04	−.11⌉	−.10	−.38*	−.20*
Severity	−.12*	−.10	−.06	−.15+	−.09	−.06	−.03
Remorse	−.12*	−.06	.03	−.09	−.31*	−.23*	−.13+
Fairness	−.16*	−.20*	−.01	−.07	−.06	−.13⌉	−.23*
Good Citizen	−.29*	−.27*	−.30*	−.18*	−.32*	−.31*	−.28*
Jobs	.04⌉	−.20*	−.09	00	−.06	−.02	−.01
In School	−.05⌉	−.03	.05	−.03	−.08	−.12	−.20*
Celerity	−.01⌉	−.02	.08	−.03	−.08	−.10	.04
Program Type (0 = tradtnl; 1 = restn)	.05+	−.04	.05	.02	.07	.02	.02
Success	−.13*	−.17+	−.21*	−.02		−.09	−.14*
Prior Offenses	.06	−.15⌉	.13+	00	.08	00	.02
In Program Subs	.06	−.02	.02	.16*	.11	.03	.08
Age	.03	−.06	−.09	.01	−.04	−.08	.09
Sex (1 = male 2 = female)	−.07*	−.17+	.08	−.12⌉	−.19*	−.16+	.02
Minority (1 = white 2 = minority)	−.04	.11	—	−.11⌉	−.06	.01	−.14+

Figures are the zero order correlation coefficients. An asterisk * indicates statistical significance less than .025; + indicates significance between .026 and .05; ⌉ shows significance between .051 and .10, two-tailed tests.

punishment was related to reduced intentions of reoffending in five of the six sites; it was statistically significant beyond 0.025 in three of them and close to significance in two others. Severity of punishment was negatively related to intentions in all six sites, but these relationships were statistically significant in only one. The small sample size precludes significance in the others, but the pattern of the relationships is relatively powerful evidence that juveniles who believe they will be punished more severely estimate their likelihood of reoffending at a lower level than do juveniles who think they will receive a milder sanction.

Although the deterrence variables had the expected effects on intentions, the best predictor of intentions to avoid crime was a self-image as a good citizen ($r = -0.29$). The sense of citizenship was measured by assessing whether the individual perceived him or herself as a person who obeys rather than disobeys rules and laws, is cooperative rather than troublesome, and is honest rather than dishonest. Good citizenship was related to lower intentions of reoffending in all six sites and was statistically significant beyond 0.001 in all six.

Persons who were more remorseful about their offense also were more adamant about their intentions to avoid crime. The sense of remorse was a scale formed by questions regarding the offender's degree of sorrow for the crime, the sense that the victim did not deserve it, the understanding that the crime was morally wrong, and the acceptance of personal responsibility for it. Persons who were more remorseful had lower intentions of reoffending in five of the six sites, and these relationships were statistically signigifcant beyond 0.05 in three of them.

Persons who believed the court process and their sanction were fair also had lower intentions to reoffend in all six places, but the relationship was statistically significant beyond 0.05 in only two of them.

Multivariate Models of Intentions to Reoffend

Self-image as a good citizen was the most important variable in understanding intentions to avoid future criminal activity ($b = -.23$, see Table 5.2). Sense of citizenship was related to lower intentions in all six sites and was well beyond the .05 level of significance in all of them. Persons who were more certain they would be caught had lower scores on intentions ($b = -.14$), as did those who believed their sanctions were more fair and those who felt more remorse. These patterns held relatively well within all of the sites (Table 5.2). Certainty of punishment was related in the expected way in five of the six sites and was significant beyond .05 in four of them. Severity of punishment, however, was significant only in Clayton County, Georgia; remorse only in Boise, Idaho, and Clayton County; and fairness only in Dane County, Wisconsin, and Ventura, California. The patterns of the relationships are probably more important than the size of the significance tests, however.

TABLE 5.2. Models of Intentions to Commit Crimes.

Dependent Variable = Intent	All Sites N=857	Ventura CA N=112	Washington D.C. N=168	Clayton County GA N=176	Boise ID N=105	Oklahoma County OK N=101	Dane County WI N=195
Certainty	−.14*	−.20+		−.11*		−.34*	−.21*
Severity				−.14*			
Remorse	−.06⌉			−.11*	−.33*		
Fair	−.06*	−.18+					−.15*
Good Citizen	−.23*	−.21*	−.29*	−.14*	−.34*	−.23*	−.20*
Jobs	−.07	−.22*			−.18+		
In School	−.05*						−.13⌉
Prior Offenses					.15+		
In Program Subs				.15			
Program							
Success in Prog.	−.08						−.15
Race (1=white, 2=minority)							−.13⌉
Sex (1=male, 2=female)	−.12+				−.15+	−.14⌉	
Age							
Adjusted R SQ	.15	.21	.08	.06	.23	.19	.20

Figures are the standardized regression coefficients (beta). An asterisk * indicates an observed significance level of .025 or less; + indicates an observed significance level between .025 and .05, and ⌉ indicates an observed signficance level between .055 and .10, on one-tailed tests. Dummy variables for the different sites were included as control variables when analyzing the pooled data. The analysis was done with SPSSx regression program. Three experential variables were controlled: program type, celerity, and successful completion of the program.

Of the background variables, only sex showed any consistent relationship, as females were less likely to say they would reoffend than were males.

Post-Release Recidivism

Correlates of Recidivism

Although the perceptual deterrence model generally performed as expected when considering intentions to commit illegal activities, the situation was vastly different when examining actual recontacts with the juvenile or adult courts during the two- or three-year followup period (See Table 5.3).

Those who acknowledged that they might commit another offense in the coming year actually committed more ($b = 0.12$), but the deterrence variables were not related to reduced offending in the manner expected. Certainty of punishment was related to subsequents in the wrong direction ($r = 0.06$, $p = 0.05$, one-tailed test); those who believed they were more likely to be caught committed more subsequent offenses. This anomaly was found in three of the six sites, but was statistically significant in only one. Perceived severity of punishment was also related to recidivism in the wrong direction ($r = .07$, $p = .05$). Higher perceptions of severity were related to greater offending in all six sites, but reached statistical significance in only two. Figures 5.1 and 5.2 graphically display the counterintuitive relationship between certainty, severity, and offense rates.

In contrast with the poor performance of the deterrence variable, self-identification as a good citizen was one of the best predictors, as persons with positive self-images were less likely to commit subsequent offenses. This relationship was found in all six sites and was statistically significant beyond .02 (one-tailed test) in all of them. The degree of remorse was related to reduced criminal activity in the pooled data ($r = -.07$, $p < .02$), and in two sites had an observed significance level below .10. Perceptions of fairness had the expected negative relationship with subsequent offenses only in Boise.

Multivariate Models of Perceptions and Recidivism

In the multivariate analysis (see Table 5.4), the good citizen self-image maintained a strong and consistent relationship with reduced offending, providing considerable strength to the notion that juveniles who do not think of themselves as criminals are much more likely to avoid crime than those who do. The extent of remorse was statistically significant in the expected direction in the pooled data and in two sites. Fairness, however, was not related to recidivism when the other variables were controlled.

TABLE 5.3. Zero Order Correlates of Subsequent Court Contacts.

	All Sites	Ventura CA	Washington D.C.	Clayton County GA.	Boise ID	Oklahoma County OK	Dane County WI
Intent	.12*	.12	.17*	.04	.29*	.18+	.06
Certainty	.06+	−.07	.13+	.11┐	−.05	−.03	.12+
Severity	.07*	.17+	.12┐	.05	.09	.04	.01
Remorse	−.07*	−.24*	.01	.06	−.24*	−.11	−.05
Fair	−.02	.03	.02	.08	−.24*	.08	.05
Citizenship	−.19*	−.21*	−.18*	−.17*	−.29*	−.23*	−.15*
Jobs	−.01	−.09	−.04	.12+	.11	−.06	−.12+
In Schools	−.09*	.22*	−.02	−.13+	−.15┐	−.15┐	.04
Celerity	−.09*	−.19*	−.08	−.15*	00	−.17*	.02
Program Type (1 = Restn; 0 = Tradtnl)	−.04	.02	−.02	.05	−.11	−.08	−.16*
Success	−.17*	−.49*	.00	−.09┐		−.27*	−.23*
Priors	.23*	.29*	.29*	.24*	.02	.23*	.34*
In Program Subs	.21*	.15*	.18*	.21*	.36*	.42*	.38*
Age	−.09*	−.21*	−.08	.06	00	−.35*	−.11┐
Sex (1 = male 2 = female)	−.12*	−.22*	−.07	−.07	−.16+	−.08	−.12+
Minority (1 = white 2 = minority)	.09*	.31*	.05	−.07	−.08	.17+	.06

Figures are the zero order correlation coefficients. Subsequents were measured from time of release to the end of the followup period; not from time of entry to the program. An asterisk * indicates statistical significance less than .025; + indicates significance between .026 and .05; ┐ shows significance between .051 and .10, two-tailed tests.

FIGURE 5.1. Annual Offense Rate and Certainty of Punishment. (The annual offense rate, per 100 youths, increased as a function of increasing certainty of punishment.)

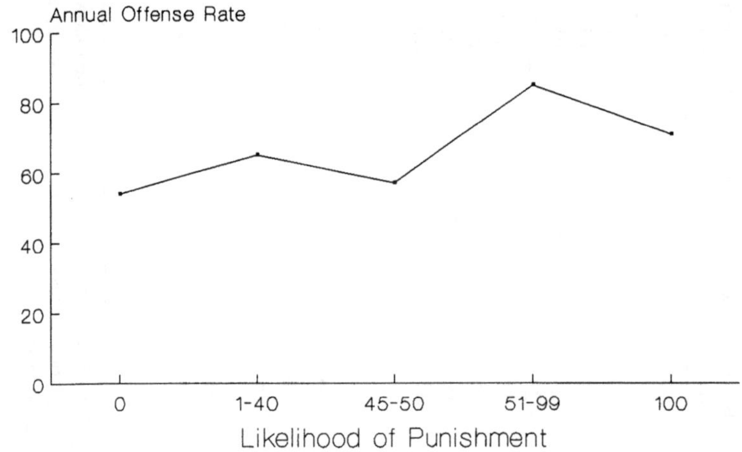

Even when all of the other variables were controlled, perceptions of certainty and severity still were not related to subsequent offenses in the manner expected by deterrence theory. Instead, persons who were more certain they would be caught were more likely to commit crimes. Perceptions of severity also had a small positive relationship to subsequents, but

FIGURE 5.2. Annual Offense Rate and Severity of Punishment. (The annual offense rate, per 100 youths, increased as a function of increasing perceived severity of punishment.)

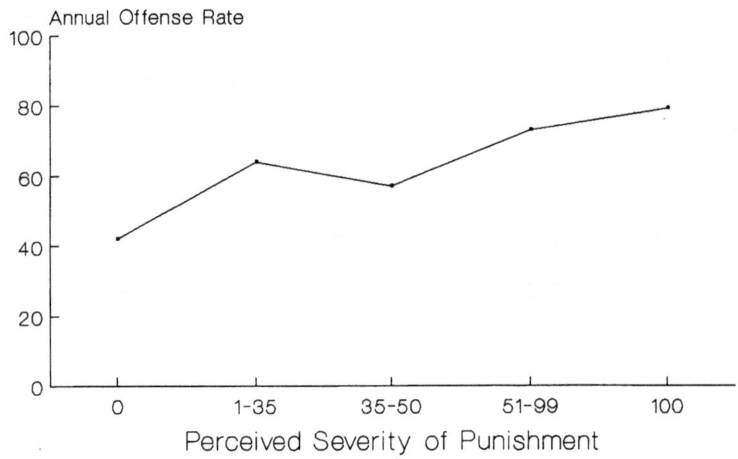

TABLE 5.4. Models of Subsequent Court Contacts.

Dependent Var. = Subsequents	All Sites N=857	Ventura CA N=112	Washington D.C. N=168	Clayton County GA N=176	Boise ID N=105	Oklahoma County OK N=101	Dane County WI N=195
Intentsions	.05+		.11*		.14⏋		
Certainty	.07+		.12⏋				
Severity							
Remorse	−.06+	−.19*			−.21*		
Fair							
Good Citizen	−.11*		−.16+	−.12+	−.16*		−.12+
Jobs							
In School	−.08*	−.19+				−.23*	
Priors	.17*	.25*		.19			.24*
In Program Subs	.13		.17	.13	.30	.34	.25
Program Type							
Success in Program	−.06	−.16					−.13
Race (1=white, 2=minority)	.14*	.15*				.18*	
Sex (1=male, 2=female)	−.09*						
Age	−.14*	−.27*				−.31*	
Adjusted R SQ	.15	.26	.06	.07	.21	.28	.21

Figures are the standardized regression coefficients for the multivariate model. Three experiential variabls also were included in the models: program type, celerity, and success in the program.

it was not statistically significant. Even so, there is absolutely no evidence in this study that offenders who are more certain they will be caught or who believe they will be punished more severely are less likely to commit crimes. The bulk of the evidence is that they will commit more crimes than others.

Decision Making and Recidivism

If decisions by juveniles to abstain from criminal behavior are not influenced much, or at all, by their perceptions of the certainty and severity of punishment, then it is important to understand why.

Methodological Issues

A host of possible methodological problems that might account for the anomalous results were first examined. More than 35 different variants of the dependent variable were examined in these models, including variables reflecting the seriousness of the offenses, different techniques for taking risk time into account, different logarithmic and clustering schemes, and different ways of dealing with risk time for incarcerated offenders. None of this made much different in the results: certainty and severity of sanctions were not related in the expected directions and often were statistically significant in the wrong directions, regardless of which version of subsequent offenses was used in the analysis. Furthermore, the zero order correlations between certainty, severity, and the various measures of outcomes were usually in the wrong direction and often statistically significant beyond the .05 level, regardless of the particular form taken by the dependent variable.

Threshold Effects

One of the most logical substantive explanations for the failure of the preceptual deterrence variables to be related in the expected way with recontacts is that the perceived likelihood of capture was so low that the severity of punishment was not relevant or that the punishment was perceived as so inconsequential that the likelihood of capture was not important.

These hypotheses were tested by examining the relationship between perceptions and subsequent behavior within different levels of the conditional variable. In Table 5.5, the sample has been divided into four groups, based on their responses to how severe they expected the penalty to be if they committed another offense. The scores were skewed toward the high side, as there were 334 who gave a score of 100, the highest possible score, to the sanction they expected to receive. In contrast, only

TABLE 5.5. Threshold Effects: Controlling Severity.

Condition:	Punishment Not Severe			Punishment Very Severe
Scale Scores:	0–50	50–76	77–99	100
N of Cases	176	102	218	334
Certainty/Subsequents	.08	−.15*	.17*	−.01
Certainty/Intentions	−.18*	−.14+	−.18*	−.15*

Figures are the zero order correlation coefficients for the pair of variables identified on the left, within each category of the conditional variable, as specified along the top.

176 persons gave scores less than 50; 102 had scores in the 50–76 range; and 218 in the 77–99 range. The bivariate correlations between perceptions of certainty and subsequent offenses, as well as stated intentions of committing crimes, were then examined within each category of severity. If certainty of punishment was important only for persons who expected the punishment to be severe, then the strongest correlation between certainty and subsequent offending should be observed for those who gave scores of 100 on the severity scale. This pattern was not found. The 334 persons who gave the highest severity scores were no more sensitive to the certainty of punishment than were the 176 persons who gave the lowest possible severity score. Further, the pattern within the two middle categories was erratic, with one group showing a statistically significant negative relationship and the other a statistically significant positive relationship.

The relationship between certainty and intentions was negative, and statistically significant at .05 or .10 for all categories of severity. This indicates that there was no threshold effect nor interaction effect between severity and certainty as they operated on intentions.

The corollary proposition, that severity of punishment becomes important only for persons who are relatively certain they will be caught, also is not supported with these data (see Table 5.6). In this analysis, the sample has been divided into five groups, based on their certainty of being

TABLE 5.6. Threshold Effects: Controlling Certainty.

Condition:	No Chance of Capture				Absolutely Certain of Capture
Scale Scores:	0	1–40	45–50	51–99	100
N of Cases	95	173	143	220	213
Severity/Subsequents	.14+	.11+	.05	.02	.04
Severity/Intentions	−.09	−.13*	−.05	−.02	−.13*

Figures are the zero order correlation coefficients for the pair of variables identified on the left, within each category of the conditional variable, as specified along the top.

caught for a subsequent offense. For the 213 persons who said there was a 100 percent probability of being caught, there was no relationship between their perception of severity and the number of subsequent offenses committed. Of the 95 persons who said there was absolutely no chance (0 probability) of being caught, those who believed they would be punished most severely were more likely to commit subsequent crimes. Clearly, the decision processes of juvenile delinquents in this study were not those envisioned by simple models of deterrence.

Good Citizen, Deterrence, Interactions

A decision heuristics theory suggests that deterrence variables may be important only for persons who seriously consider criminal activity—namely, those who view themselves as lawbreakers. Persons who consider themselves good citizens do not frame situations in such a way as to recognize criminal opportunities when they occur; they are less likely to search for ideas about how to commit crimes; and they are less likely to envision scenarios in which they are successful in a criminal enterprise. Persons whose self-image is that of a lawbreaker, on the other hand, are expected to look for criminal opportunities, or at least to recognize them when they occur; they envision themselves committing offenses and being successful at it; and they are expected to assess the possible gains and risk level, even though this may be highly inaccurate (Cornish & Clarke, 1986). If so, then perceptions of certainty and severity should be important for persons who see themselves as lawbreakers, but not for good citizens.

These ideas were examined by dividing the sample into several different categories on the good citizenship variable (see Table 5.7). If the deterrence perceptions were mainly relevant only for those who viewed themselves as lawbreakers, then the correlations should be close to zero for the good citizens and gradually become negative moving across the scale toward lawbreaker. This pattern was not observed for actual recontacts with the court. However, as has been true elsewhere in the data,

TABLE 5.7. Threshold Effects: Controlling Self-Image.

Condition:	Good Citizen				Law Breaker
Scale:	7-6.9	6.8-5.5	5.4-4.6	4.5-3.6	3.5-1.0
N of Cases	176	157	186	177	150
Certainty/Subsequents	.03	.05	.14*	.08*	.02
Severity/Subsequents	.06	.21*	.10+	−.01	.14*
Certainty/Intentions	−.06	−.02	−.15*	−.19*	−.26*
Severity/Intentions	.02	−.14*	−.14*	−.14*	−.09*

Figures are the zero order correlation coefficients for the pair of variables identified on the left, within each category of the conditional variable, as specified along the top.

the pattern clearly holds for the relationship between certainty and intentions to commit crimes. For the two groups with the highest scores on good citizenship, there was no relationship between certainty and intentions; but this turned negative (−.15) for the middle group and increased to −.26 for the group with the most extreme lawbreaker self-image. Severity of punishment was not relevant for the good citizens, but was negatively related for all the other groups, providing some weak support for the contention that severity was more important for those with lawbreaker images than for those who viewed themselves as good citizens.

Decay Effects

Another possible reason for the finding that perceptions of certainty and severity were related in the expected manner to intentions to commit crimes but not to actual subsequent courts contacts during the followup period is that the effects of these perceptions might decay over time. As was clear from the descriptive data presented earlier, juveniles in this study were quite certain they would be caught if they reoffended and most believed they would be punished severely. But if these perceptions decay, once the youths are out of the juvenile justice system, they would have little effect on later criminal activity. To test these ideas, the strength of the relationship between certainty, severity, and reoffending was examined for the first month after release from the program, the second month, a six-month time lag, and the full followup period (see Table 5.8). For this analysis, no correction for risk time was included in the dependent variables.

If perceptions of certainty and severity influence offending immediately upon release but lose their impact later, the correlations should be especially strong for the first time lag and gradually weaken as the lag time becomes longer. The zero order correlations shown in Table 5.8 indicate

TABLE 5.8. Immediacy Effects of Certainty And Severity.

	Lag 1	Lag 2	Lag 6	All Subsequents
Certainty	.00	.00	.00	.06
Severity	.04	.05	.04	.05
Remorse	.00	−.03	−.07*	−.07*
Fairness	.00	−.03	−.05	−.02
Intent	.07*	.10*	.09*	.12*
Good Citizen	−.10*	−.13*	−.14*	−.21*

Figures are the zero order correlation coefficients for subsequent offenses committed during specific time periods. Lag 1 counts only subsequents committed during the first month after release; lag 2 counts subsequents for the first and second months; lag six includes subsequents for months 1 through six. Logged values of the dependent variable were used in the analysis.

no support for this contention with either certainty or severity of punishment.

It is very interesting, however, that remorse appears to have more effect for the longer time lags, as does the good citizen variable. One interpretation of these findings is that the ethical bases of decision making are a stronger and more enduring predictor of actual behavior than are perceptions of gains and losses. Perceptions of certainty and severity do not decay with time; a better explanation is that these perceptions change with circumstances and are shaped primiarly by the circumstances of the moment, rather than by stable or long-standing beliefs.

The "Macho" Explanation

Another explanation for the fact that certainty and severity did not work as expected is that some juveniles adopt a "macho" attitude toward crime, viewing it as fun, exciting, brave, and dangerous. These are side benefits of illegal activity: "thrills." These same persons may overestimate the certainty of capture and severity of punishment because they are positively attracted to risky ventures. Thus, the failure of perceived certainty and severity to correlate in the expected manner with subsequent offenses might be attributed to the fact that the "macho" attitudes, or "thrills" were not controlled in the statistical analysis. These possibilities were tested by using questions on the survey in which the juveniles were asked about their attitudes toward the crime they had committed in terms of whether it was "brave" or "cowardly," "exciting" or "dull," "fun" or "boring," and "dangerous" or "safe." Inclusion of the "thrills" variables in the multivariate equations did not alter the relationships of certainty or severity (or any of the other predictors).

Table 5.9 shows the zero order correlations between the "thrills" variables and selected other variables. All four were related to intentions to commit subsequent crimes, with persons who thought the crime was brave, exciting, and fun being more inclined to say they would commit another offense, and those who said the offense was dangerous being less inclined to do so. There were no relationships, however, with actual subsequents.

TABLE 5.9. "Macho" Explanations.

	Loutsub	Intent	Certain	Severe	Citizen
Brave	.04	.10*	−.14	−.10	−.06
Exciting	.02	.13*	−.10	−.06	−.14
Fun	.04	.15*	−.09	−.10	−.20
Danger	− 04	−.12*	.12*	.14*	.16*

Figures are the zero order correlation coefficients. An * indicates significance beyond .05, one-tailed test.

Curvilinear Effects

To examine whether the relationship between certainty, severity, and reoffending might be obscured through curvilinear effects, the annualized offense rates within several categories of severity and certainty were examined (see Table 5.10). For the pooled data, the number of offenses obviously increased as estimates of certainty increased, contrary to deterrence theory, and then dropped off slightly for persons who believed there was a 100 percent probability of being caught. Within the six sites, only in Ventura was the pattern clearly one in which reoffending declined as certainty of punishment increased. The proportion of offenders who had at least one recontact with the court shows virtually the same pattern as the annual rates.

Reoffending also increased as perceptions of the severity of punishment increased. This pattern held in most of the sites. Only in Oklahoma County was there a declining pattern in which reoffending rates declined as perceptions of the severity of punishment increased.

TABLE 5.10. Curvilinear Effects.

	All Sites N=857	Ventura CA N=112	Washington D.C. N=168	Clayton County GA N=176	Boise ID N=105	Oklahoma County OK N=101	Dane County WI N=195
	ANNUAL OFFENSE RATES						
Certain							
0	.39	.90	.39	.24	.15	.45	.29
1–50	.53	.65	.50	.44	.62	.72	.45
51–99	.68	.85	.69	.57	.48	.85	.73
100	.56	.43	.91	.46	.65	.55	.45
Score							
0	.35	—	.33	—	—	—	.71
1–50	.48	.52	.34	.34	.37	.11	.54
51–99	.57	.73	.65	.46	.56	.79	.39
100	.60	.80	.61	.52	.69	.39	.63
	PROPORTION REOFFENDING (PREVALENCE)						
	%	%	%	%	%	%	%
Score							
0	43	—	—	—	—	—	67
1–50	48	54	33	47	50	37	52
51–99	52	67	54	45	49	57	49
100	49	68	52	41	60	39	41
Certain							
0	45	77	50	30	33	50	40
1–50	49	69	43	43	63	50	43
51–99	55	67	55	48	49	59	61
100	46	47	56	45	47	39	46

In the upper portion of the table are the annual offense rates for each category of certainty and severity. In the lower portion of the table are the proportion reoffending, for each category of certainty and severity.

Deterrence and Experienced Offenders

It may be the case that perceptions of certainty and severity are most important only for naive, rather than experienced, offenders. Alternatively, one might argue that naive offenders have not developed stable estimates of certainty or severity of punishment, and therefore their perceptions at the time of the interview would not be good predictors of their behavior over the next two years. Experienced offenders, on the other hand, may have developed more realistic views of certainty and severity, and these would have more predictive power for them.

The data in Table 5.11 show the zero order correlations between subsequents and the independent variables, for persons with different numbers of prior contacts. One of the interesting revelations from this analysis is that relationships between severity of punishment and subsequent offending clearly follow a pattern: First offenders who believed they would be punished more severely were more likely to commit subsequents than were persons who believed they would not be punished as severely (r = .12). Moving across the levels of experience, however, this relationship dropped to .05, .04, −.09, and then to −.23 for the persons with six or more priors. The clear indication here is that perceptions of severity were important in suppressing delinquency only for very experienced offenders. A similar pattern was not observed for perceptions of certainty, how-

TABLE 5.11. Naive and Experienced Offenders.

	ZERO ORDER CORRELATIONS WITHIN CATEGORIES OF PRIORS				
	0 priors N=333	1 prior N=197	2–3 priors N=200	4 or more N = 127	6 or more N = 58
Intent	.04	.11*	.19*	.13	.12
Certain	.05	.07	.05	−.01	.05
Score	.12*	.05	.04	−.09	−.23*
Remorse	.02	−.14*	−.15*	−.09	−.01
Fair	−.09*	.04	.03	−.02	−.10
Good Citizen	−.11*	−.22*	−.10+	−.32*	−.26*
Restitution	−.09*	.07	00	−.07	−.02
Incarcrtd	.12*	00	.06	.03	−.14
# Days Incarc	.13*	.08	−.06	.16*	.07
% formal		−.15*	.05	−.14	−.06
Celerity	−.14*	.08	−.11*	−.04	.18
Seriousness of offense	.12*	00	−.10+	−.05	−.07
No job	−.13*	.10	00	.03	−.09
Employed	.04	.03	−.07	−.03	.03
School	.02	.06	−.08	−.14	−.14
Age	−.09*	−.12*	−.19*	−.21*	−.28*
Sex	−.15*	−.01	−.10	−.19*	−.14
Minority	.10*	.06	.10	.11	00

ever. Self-image as a good citizen was negatively related to subsequent offending within all of the different categories, including the most experienced offenders.

Deterrence and Type of Crime

One of the possible reasons that perceptual deterrence models do not perform well when predicting subsequent offenses is that perceptions may be relatively specific to certain types of offenses. In the current study, respondents were asked to assess the likelihood of stealing something worth more than $20 in the next year. This became the offense that was referenced in further questioning about the certainty of being caught and the severity of punishment. Thus, it may be the case that perceptions of certainty and severity will be more strongly related to crimes that are more similar to those referenced in the interview.

The data in Table 5.12 indicate that the perceptual variables work in about the same way for trivial, property, and personal offenders. The certainty of punishment was not related to subsequent offending or was positively related, as was the expected severity of punishment. Remorse was negatively related for both property and personal offenders. Persons who believed they were good citizens were less likely to commit subsequents, regardless of the type of offense.

TABLE 5.12. Deterrence Models for Types of Offenders.

	Trivial N=150	Prop N=594	Personal N=81
Intent	.10	.12	.16
Certain	00	.06	.03
Score	.07	.07	.04
Remorse	00	.10	.08
Fair	.02	.05	.03
Good Citizen	.20	.19	.11
Restitution	.07	.06	.02
# Days Incarcerated	.13	.14	.27
Formal Sanctions	.24	.17	.03
Celerty	.06	.08	.15
Priors	.38	.22	.08
No Job	.06	.03	.06
Employee	.12	.03	.13
School	.06	.11	.06
Age	.07	.08	.13
Sex	.12	.12	.07
Minority	.10	.14	.04

Discussion

Analysis of perceptions, values, and recidivism in the six cities studied here provide far more support for decision heuristic theories that grant a dominant role to basic values and self-images than to deterrence theory that focuses on perceptions of certainty or severity of punishment. The fact that perceptions of certainty and severity of punishment could be so irrelevant to future decisions, however, also may indicate the primacy of contextual influences on perceptions. Normative and ethical orientations may guide the manner in which individuals frame and define situations, and may be instrumental in where they search for ideas as well as those given serious considerations. It makes sense to believe that good citizens do not even recognize most crime opportunities, much less devise imaginary scenarios about how they might be successful in committing them. If normative orientations do not screen out certain actions, then the perceptions of gains, losses, and risks may be important, but may not be particularly accurate, stable, or general except for the most experienced offenders. Perceptions may depend more heavily on context; ideas about the certainty of capture and severity of punishment may change dramatically whenever a specific crime opportunity is considered. The opportunity may be evaluated either as a "sure thing" (and carried out) or as a certain loss (and foregone). The threshold analysis suggests that perceptions of certainty and severity were essentially irrelevant to whether self-identified good citizens intended to commit future crimes, but were more important in shaping the intentions of lawbreakers. And the perceptions of punishment severity were more strongly related to actual subsequent contacts as a function of the previous criminal experience of the individual.

In general, this research finds much support for the decision heuristic models such as those proposed by the authors in Cornish & Clarke (1986) and very little support for the strictly rational models upon which traditional deterrence theory is based.

6
Direct Effects of Programs on Recidivism

The findings from the previous chapter do not bode well for punishment policies, with the possible exception of their importance for the most chronic and serious offenders. If perceptions of certainty and severity of punishment influence intentions regarding reoffending, but have little or nothing to do with subsequent criminal behavior, then it is unlikely that programs emphasizing the fear factor will be effective. These programs may seem to hold the promise of reducing delinquency because they are believed to induce an immediate intent of avoiding crime; but the context within which actual decisions to commit crimes are made differ substantially from the context in which those intentions are shaped by programmatic experiences. The findings that one's sense of citizenship and remorse are more important in understanding recidivism offer hope for advocates of probation and restitution. Before examining the effect of programs on perceptions, however, it is important to first establish the direct effects—if any exist—between the type of program and subsequent recidivism rates. Programs may impact recidivism for all sorts of reasons that are not covered in this study. Thus, this chapter focuses on the direct linkage between program type and recidivism.

Although the analysis is based on field experiments in six cities located throughout the United States, field experiments are seldom perfect and do not involve the tight controls found in the laboratory. For this reason, the data need to be examined from a number of different perspectives. Direct effects on recidivism can be estimated by examining whether the programs suppressed the offense rate, producing lower rates after intervention than before, as well as by comparing the postprogram offense rates across the random assignment conditions. Random assignment into different programs permits comparisons of restitution programs with incarceration, traditional probation, and the ad hoc approach to restitution found in some juvenile justice systems. There were no direct comparisons of traditional probation (i.e., probation without restitution orders) and incarceration. It should be reemphasized, however, that juveniles in the restitution programs were on probation, but the probation programs were oriented around the restitution requirements rather than around traditional counseling approaches.

The dependent variables used in this chapter are LSUB1, which is the number of subsequent offenses after entry to the program, corrected for time at risk, and logged to reduce skewness; ANYSUB, the proportion who commit one or more offense after program entry; and LSSER1, the seriousness scale representing both seriousness of offenses and number of offenses, corrected for time at risk, and logged to reduce skewness. All offenses that occurred after the date of referral to the program are counted as subsequents, including those that were committed while the youths were in the program, on the grounds that programs should be responsible for offenses committed while the juveniles are under court jurisdiction as well as those committed after they leave. Even the offenses committed by juveniles while they were incarcerated are included. For this reason, the time spent in institutions is included as part of the overall risk time. Violations of probation, failure to complete restitution requirements, and other technical violations are not counted as crimes in any of the analyses.

Suppression Effects

Suppression effects were estimated by comparing the annual offense rate for each youth prior to intervention with the annual offense rates after intervention. The immediate offense that brought the youth into the program was omitted from the analysis. The results are shown in Table 6.1 and in Figure 6.1.

Program Effects

Juveniles in Group 1, RESINC, were eligible for incarceration and were randomly assigned between restitution and incarceration. Both of these interventions had a suppression effect of about the same magnitude (Table 6.1 and Figure 6.1). The preprogram rate averaged 1.2 crimes per juvenile per year for both the probation and incarceration groups, whereas the postprogram rates were 0.81 for the incarceration group and 0.88 for the restitution group. The observed significance levels of .10 and .06, respectively (two-tailed tests), indicate the changes probably are attributable to program impact rather than to chance variation in the data.

The RESINC group included cases from both Boise and Ventura. Examining these programs separately reveals two different patterns. In Boise, the incarceration experience had a more marked suppression effect than the restitution experience, and was statistically significant, whereas the suppression effect produced by the restitution program was

TABLE 6.1. Suppression Effects.

	No. Cases	Prior Rate (Annual)	Subsequent Rate (Annual)	Observed Significance Level
ALL CASES				
Traditional	286	.97	.80	.08
Restitution	569	.82	.64	.00
GROUP I RESINC				
Incarceration	79	1.2	.81	.10
Restitution	97	1.2	.88	.06
GROUP 2 RESPRO				
Probation	140	.75	.82	.56
Restitution	269	.65	.58	.32
GROUP 3 RESAD				
AdHoc Restn.	65	1.19	.76	.05
Restitution	203	.87	.59	.00
SITE SPECIFIC COMPARISONS				
BOISE				
Incarceration	41	1.29	.73	.04
Restitution	64	.98	.89	.75
WASH DC				
Incarceration	[3]	[.33]	[.59]	
Restitution	33	1.0	.82	.29
VENTURA				
Incarceration	12	.79	1.29	.08
Restitution	35	1.7	.96	.02
WASH D.C.				
Probation	68	.57	.66	.42
Restitution	48	.58	.48	.29
CLAYTON CO.				
Probation	71	.80	.91	.59
Restitution	105	.76	.61	.24
OKLAHOMA CO.				
Probation	32	.87	.82	.81
Restitution	69	.57	.67	.46
DANE COUNTY				
Ad Hoc Restn	49	1.4	.77	.02
Restitution	45	.90	.49	.00
VENTURA				
Ad Hoc Restn	16	.53	.72	.40
Restitution	58	.79	.86	.66

Suppression effects are judged by comparing the pre and post offense rates. Tests of significance (two-tailed, t-test) pertain to the pre/post comparison for each program. Group 1 cases were eligible for incarceration and were randomly assigned either into incarceration or into probation. Data for this comparison came from Boise, Ventura, and Washington D.C. Group 2 cases were eligible for probation, and were randomly assigned either into probation or restitution. Date for Group 2 cases were from Clayton County, Oklahoma County, and Washington, D.C. Group 3 cases had court-ordered restitution, and were randomly assigned either to a restitution program or to a probation program. Data for Group 3 were from Dane County Wisconsin and Ventura California. In the upper portions of the table, the pooled data are displayed; in the lower portions are the results from each random assignment condition within each site.

FIGURE 6.1a. Incarceration and Restitution: Effect on Recidivism. (Both incarceration and restitution show statistically significant suppression effects.)

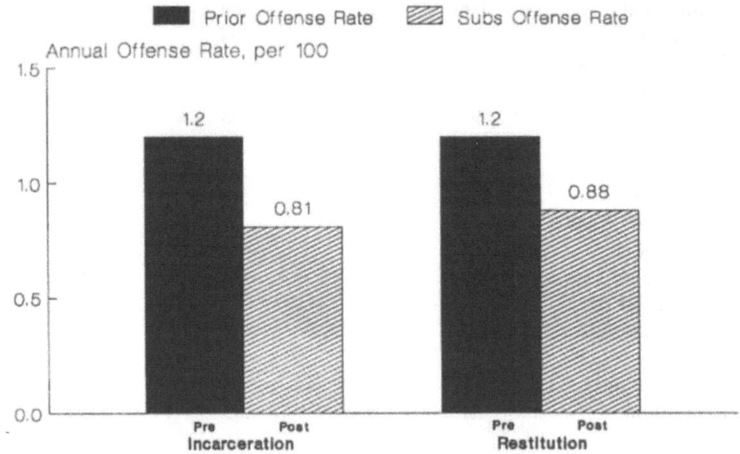

not. The situation was quite different in Ventura, however, where the incarceration experience was associated with a marked increase in recidivism, compared with the restitution experience, which produced a marked decline. Both these differences were statistically significant beyond 0.10.

The RESPRO group (Group 2) was formed from random experiments in which persons eligible for probation were randomly assigned into pro-

FIGURE 6.1b. Probation and Restitution: Effect on Recidivism. (Juveniles in the restitution programs reduced their offense rate; those in probation increased their rate.)

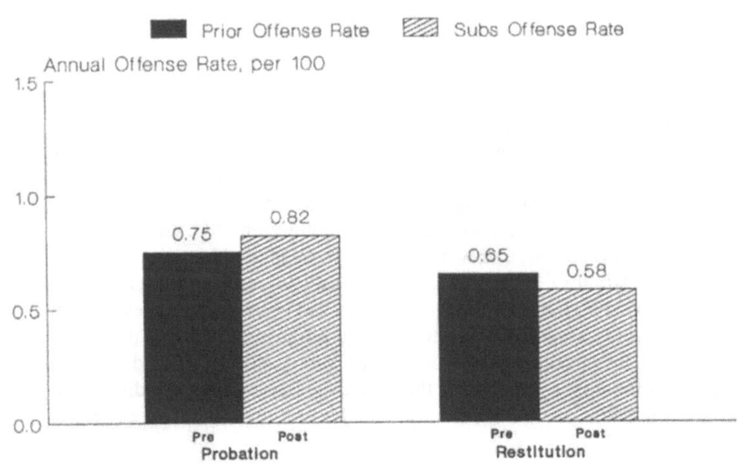

FIGURE 6.1c. Ad Hoc and Restitution: Effects on Recidivism. (Both interventions show suppression effects.)

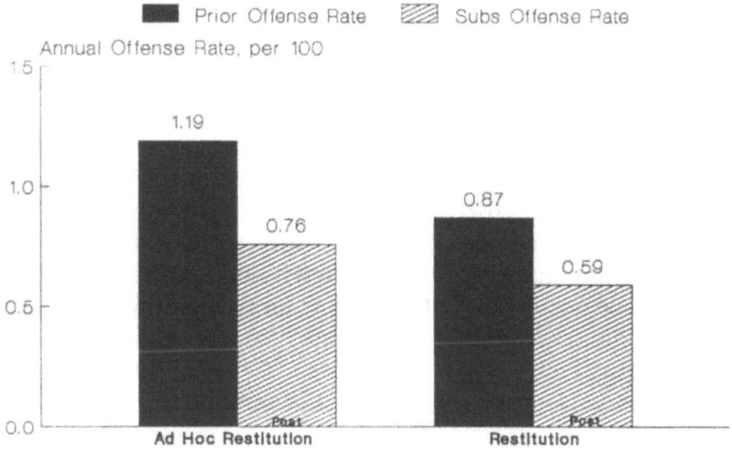

bation or restitution. These results reveal that neither restitution nor probation had a suppression effect. The rate actually increased slightly for the probation group and decreased slightly for the restitution group, but both changes may well have occurred by chance alone (o.s.1. of .56 and .32, respectively, two-tailed tests). Examination of suppression effects for the three experiments that produced data for the probation versus restitution analysis indicates that no statistically significant suppression

FIGURE 6.1d. Restitution and All Controls: Effects on Recidivism. (Restitution shows a slightly greater suppression effect and a lower post-program offense rate.)

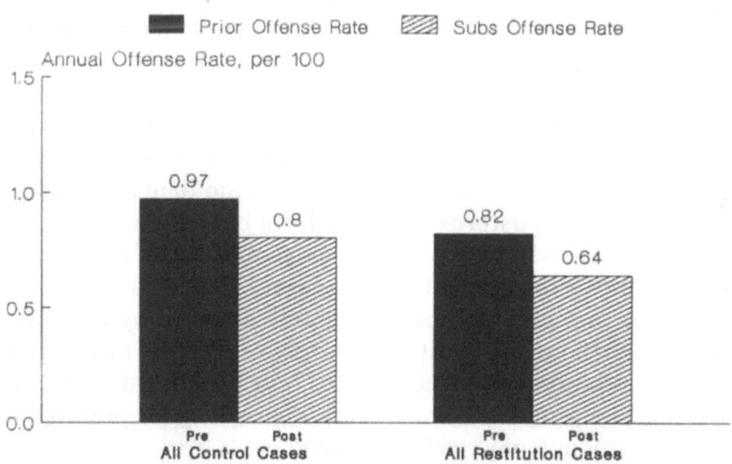

effects occurred in any of them. In Washington, the probation group actually showed a slight increase and the restitution group a slight decrease, but neither was statistically significant. In Clayton Country, the same pattern was observed (probation increased and restitution decreased) but the differences were not great enough to rule out chance as the probable cause. In Oklahoma Country, probation showed a slight decline and restitution a slight increase, but neither was statistically significant.

The comparison of two types of restitution—programmatic and ad hoc—revealed that both had marked suppression effects. For the ad hoc group, the rate dropped from 1.19 to .76 and for the regular restitution program, it dropped from .87 to .59. Both were statistically significant beyond .05. Examination of these data within sites indicates that the substantial impact occurred in the Dane County experiment where the relatively high preprogram rates of 1.4 and .90, for ad hoc and regular restitution, respectively, were reduced to .77 and .49. Ventura actually showed an increase for both groups, but neither was statistically significant.

When all of the restitution cases are aggregated and compared with all control conditions (see Figure 6.1, Table 6.1), both show statistically significant suppression effects of about the same magnitude and both changes were statistically significant. For all restitution cases, the offense rate dropped from .82 per year during the two-year preprogram period to .64 per year for the followup. For all control cases the drop was from 0.97 to .80 per year.

Discussion of Suppression Effects

Suppression effects are interesting, but there are some potential problems in interpreting them. In particular, there is the possibility that groups with unnaturally high preprogram rates will regress toward the mean in the postprogram period, not because of program impact, but simply because behavioral phenomenon naturally vary, over time, for all sorts of reasons. Groups that happened to be unusually high in the postprogram period will drop toward their actual mean, thereby producing a pseudo-effect. Furthermore, rates that were higher in the preprogram period have further to fall. This problem is especially acute in analysis of offense rates. If only one very high rate offender in the preprogram time period abandons criminal behavior, the postprogram period will be substantially lower. Finally, it is not clear whether the analysis should focus on the absolute amount of decline or the percentage decrease. In the data shown in Table 6.1, the offense rate for traditional programs declined by 0.17 offenses, compared with 0.18 for the restitution programs; but the rate of decrease was 0.22 for restitution compared with 0.17 for traditional programs. For these reasons, postprogram comparisons, controlling for preprogram differences, may produce more reliable results.

Post-Program Comparisons

Comparisons of offense rates and prevalance rates are shown in Table 6.2. The results here generally favored the restitution group over the probation controls and showed no difference between restitution and incarceration. When all restitution cases were compared against all controls, the difference in annual offense rates (0.64 versus 0.80) was statistically significant, as was the percentage reoffending (57% versus 64%). When restitution was compared with incarceration, however, there were no statistically significant differences and the incarcerated group actually had lower rates in both cases. The comparison of probation with restitution revealed that restitution had lower offense and prevalence rates, with the latter statistically significant at 0.02. The comparison of ad hoc restitution with restitution also favored the programmatic restitution, with the difference in prevalance rate significant at 0.00 and the different in subsequents had a 0.19 observed significance level (two-tailed test).

Within the sites, the results seldom showed statistical significance due to the relatively small number of cases, but the pattern consistently favored restitution except for the experiments in which restitution was compared directly with incarceration. In these, there were no differences.

Figures 6.2 and 6.3 graphically portray these results. Annual offense rates (Figure 6.2) for restitution were slightly higher than for incarcerated cases, but for the probation comparison, ad hoc comparison, and overall

TABLE 6.2. Offense Rates and Prevalence Rates for Post-Program Comparisons.

		Percent Reoffending		Subsequent Rate (Annual)	
	No Cases	%	o.s.1	Rate	o.s.1.
ALL CASES					
Traditional	286	64%	.05	.80	.03
Restitution	569	57%		.64	
GROUP 1 RESINC					
Incarceration	79	63%	.35	.81	.68
Restitution	97	69%		.88	
GROUP 2 RESPRO					
Probation	140	60%	.34	.82	.02
Restitution	269	55%		.58	
GROUP 3 RESAD					
AdHoc Restn.	65	76%	.00	.76	.19
Restitution	203	54%		.59	
SITE SPECIFIC COMPARISONS					
BOISE					
Incarceration	41	59%	.87	.73	.59
Restitution	64	61%		.89	

TABLE 6.2. (*cont.*)

	No Cases	Percent Reoffending		Subsequent Rate (Annual)	
		%	o.s.1	Rate	o.s.1.
WASH DC					
Incarceration	[3]	[33%]		[.59]	
Restitution	33	64%		.82	
VENTURA					
Incarceration	12	91%	.97	1.29	.32
Restitution	35	91%		.96	
WASH D.C.					
Probation	68	65%	.29	.66	.18
Restitution	48	55%		.48	
CLAYTON CO.					
Probation	71	59%	.70	.91	.13
Restitution	105	56%		.61	
OKLAHOMA CO.					
Probation	32	56%	.81	.82	.49
Restitution	69	54%		.67	
DANE COUNTY					
Ad Hoc Restn	49	78%	.00	.77	.06
Restitution	45	45%		.49	
VENTURA					
Ad Hoc Restn	16	75%	.83	.72	.55
Restitution	58	78%		.86	

Figures show the offense rates and the prevalence rates (proportion reoffending) for the post-program comparisons. Tests of significance (two-tailed, t-tests) show the probability that differences in type of program are related to differences in offense rates or prevalence rates in the post-program period. Group 1 cases were eligible for incarceration and were randomly assigned either into incarceration or into probation. Data for this comparison came from Boise, Ventura, and Washington D.C. Group 2 cases were eligible for probation, and were randomly assigned either into probation or restitution. Data for Group 2 cases were from Clayton County, Oklahoma County, and Washington, D.C. Group 3 cases had court-ordered restitution, and were randomly assigned either to a restitution program or to a probation program. Data for Group 3 were from Dane County Wisconsin and Ventura California. In the upper portions of the table, the pooled data are displayed; in the lower portions are the results from each random assignment condition within each site.

comparison, the restitution programs had lower rates. Analysis of the proportion reoffending (Figure 6.3) shows precisely the same pattern, with restitution having slightly higher reoffense rates, but lower rates for the other comparisons and for the pooled data.

One of the problems with direct postprogram comparisons, of course, is that there were some differences in priors and demographic characteristics of juveniles in the programs. Although these were seldom statistically

FIGURE 6.2. Annual Offense Rates of Randomly Assigned Cases. (The differences are statistically signifant (.05, one-tailed test) except for the incarceration vs. restitution group.)

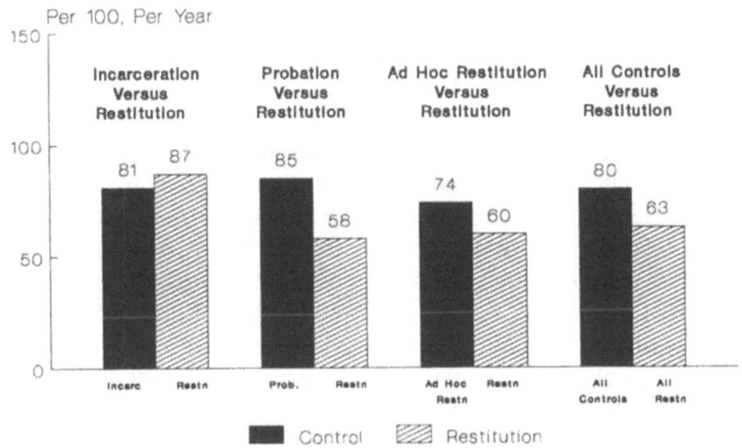

significant, it is important to examine program effects controlling for differences in priors, age, race, and sex. The dependent variables in this analysis include not only the offense rate and prevalance rate, but also a seriousness scale that weights each subsequent offense with its relative seriousness and sums these to form one overall indicator of crime seriousness.

FIGURE 6.3. Percent Reoffending Among Randomly Assigned Cases. (All differences are statistically significant beyond .05 (one-tailed test) except for Restitution vs. Incarceration)

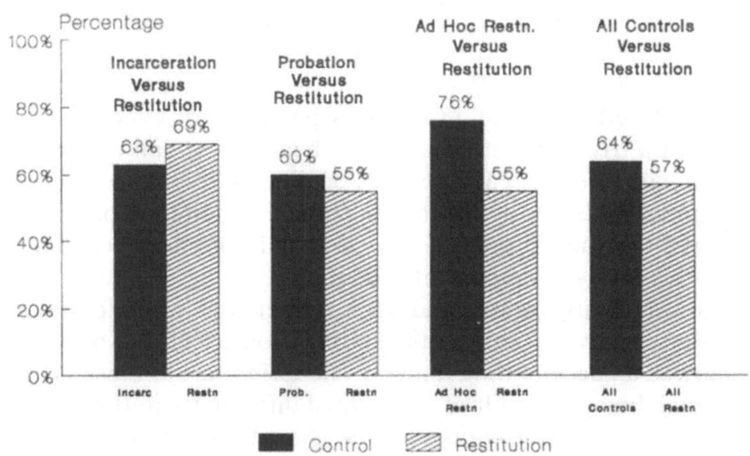

The multivariate analysis controlling for priors and other possibly confounding variables (Table 6.3) reinforces the results reported with the direct comparisons. For all cases combined, restitution programs had lower offense rates, prevalance rates, and lower scores on the seriousness scale. The zero order correlations were −0.07 for all three and were statistically significant. When the other variables were controlled, the regression coefficient dropped to −0.06 for the offense and prevalence rates, and stayed at −0.07 for the seriousness scale. The multivariate analysis indicates that there were no differences between restitution and incarceration when priors and other demographic characteristics were controlled. Significant differences were found for the restitution versus probation comparison, however. For the ad hoc restituiton versus programmatic restitution, the regression coefficients with the other variables controlled were −0.07, −0.17, and −0.07 for offense rate, prevalence rate, and seriousness scale, respectively. The −0.07 rates had observed significance levels of 0.105 and almost certainly represent true program effects rather than chance variation.

Discussion of Direct Effects

Several issues are raised with this analysis. First, do interventions reduce offense rates and are these reductions large enough to be important from a policy perspective? If it is assumed that suppression effects represent program impacts rather than regression to the mean, then the pattern of results indicates that almost any type of intervention may have a suppression effect, but the implementation and operational characteristics of the program probably are more important than the type of program itself. In the eight restitution comparisons reported here, the postprogram offense rate was lower than the preprogram rate in six of the eight tests and these were statistically significant twice. In the other two, the slight increases in the postprogram rate were almost certainly the result of chance variation. Thus, the data show that restitution programs sometimes reduced recidivism, never had a negative effect, and in other instances did not have permanent or long-term effects on offense rates. Overall, restitution programs produced a drop of 18 offenses per year for every 100 juveniles. This is not a trivial effect. A city of a half million can expect 10,000 or more juvenile referrals each year. A decline of 18 offenses per year, per 100 juveniles adds up to 1800 fewer crimes. Traditional programs, when considered together, produced a decline of 17 offenses per year, per 100 youths; this too is an important reduction.

Of the two incarceration conditions with enough cases for analysis, the one in Boise showed a substantial suppression effect, but the one in Ventura showed an accelerating impact. The difference in these programs almost certainly is the result of substantial differences in the type of incarceration program. Boise operated a short-term detention program in

TABLE 6.3. Direct Program Effects on Recidivism, Controlling for Possible Confounding Variables.

	Offense Rate		Prevalance Rate		Seriousness Scale	
	r	b	r	b	r	b
ALL CASES (N = 857)						
Program 0 = trad 1 = restn	−.07*	−.06*	−.07*	−.06*	−.07*	−.07*
Priors	.32*	.31*	.26*	.24*	.30*	.30*
Seriousness	.31*		.25*		.31*	
Age	−.07	−.13*	−.03	−.08	−.07*	−.14*
Minority	.05+	.14*	.02		.12*	.15*
Female	−.12*	−.11*	−.11*	−.10*	−.14*	−.11*
R2		.14		.11		.15
RESINC (N = 140)						
Program 0 = trad 1 = restn	.04		.08		.00	
Priors	.15*	55*	.17*	.11*	.14*	
Seriousness	.12*	−.44*	.15*		.12*	
Age	.05		.14*		.06	
Minority	.22*	.22*	.12+		.25*	.20*
Female	−.11*		−.22*	−.17*	−.15*	−.11*
R2		.06		.11		.08
RESPRO (N = 409)						
Program 0 = trad 1 = restn	−.09*	−.07*			−.09*	−.09*
Priors	.32*	.33*	.22*	.23*	.30*	.31*
Seriousness	.31*		.21*		.30*	
Age	−.06	−.12*	−.04*	−.08*	−.06	−.15*
Minority	−.00		.03		.06	.07*
Female	−.09*	−.11*	−.06	−.07*	−.12*	−.13*
R2		.13		.05		.12
RESAD (N = 268)						
Program 0 = trad 1 = restn	−.13*	[−.07]	−.20*	−.17*	−.12*	[−.07]
Priors	.40*	.39*	.32*	.32*	.39*	.38*
Seriousness	.39*		.32*		.39*	
Age	−.16*	−.15*	−.08		−.15*	−.14*
Minority	.21*	.14*	.10		.23*	.16*
Female	−.18*	−.09	−.16*		−.18*	−.09*
R2						

Measures of recidivism shown across the top are LSUB1, ANYSUB. and LSSER1. Figures in the first column under each variable are the zero order correlation coefficient. The standardized regression coefficient (b) is shown in the second column under each variable. An asterisk * indicates statistical significance beyond .05 (one-tailed test); + indicates significance between .05 and .20 (one-tailed test). Figures shown in brackets are the standardized regression coefficient for a variable that is not in the equation. These are shown for informational purposes only.

which juveniles were incarcerated for a series of weekends. On average, the extent of detention was 8.4 days. The youths remained on probation after the detention time had been served. Ventura's program was a more traditional institutional setting in which the juveniles were removed from their homes and placed in secure or semisecure residential settings. It also should be pointed out that the restitution program in Ventura involved a nonsecure residential setting, where juveniles were housed at night but were free during the day to attend school and work.

Of the three traditional probation programs (Washington, D.C., Clayton County, and Oklahoma County), none had any demonstrable effect on offense rates, and even when the cases wre combined, there was no suppression effect. Two probation programs showed statistically insignificant upward shifts and one showed an insignificant downward shift. For the two examples of ad hoc restitution, in which restitution sanctions were imposed within the context of a traditional probation program, one showed a statistically significant decline but the other showed no effect.

A reasonable conclusion here is that almost any kind of program may produce suppression effects, but restitution programs are somewhat more likely to do so than other dispositions, and traditional probation programs are least likely to show suppression effects. Nevertheless, the fact should not be lost that suppression effects depend importantly on site-specific program characteristics. If restitution programs are slightly more likely to have suppression effects, this may be because restitution is somewhat easier to implement and operate in an effective manner. Restitution programs may be less dependent upon the characteristics of program personnel than are traditional probation programs. After all, restitution programs depend upon the juvenile's work supervisor for much of the day-to-day supervision. Restitution programs also are more inclined to break old patterns of association and to physically occupy the leisure time of the youths with work either in the private or public sector. Thus, restitution programs introduce more changes in the juvenile's day-to-day activities than traditional programs do. Still, there is no guarantee that restitution will produce suppression effects, just as there is no guarantee that incarceration will reduce offense rates rather than increase them.

The second issue is whether restitution programs produced greater impacts than the traditional programs against which they were compared. The results here are relatively consistent. First, restitution programs had lower offense, prevalance, and seriousness rates than probation programs for the pooled data and within all three programs where these comparisons were made. Second, there were no differences between restitution and incarceration in the pooled data, in Boise, Idaho, or in Ventura, California. Third, programmatic restitution enjoyed a distinct advantage over ad hoc restitution in Dane County, Wisconsin, but there were no differences between these two in Ventura, California.

Again, the results show that restitution programs may be more robust than probation, in the sense that they tend to be more effective under a variety of conditions, but the implementation and operation of specific programs are important enough that one cannot expect programs of a particular type to always outperform other kinds of programs.

In the next chapter, the analysis turns to why and how program experiences influence perceptions or other variables and how these, in turn, influence recidivism.

7 Experiences, Perceptions, and Recidivism

The six experimental studies show that restitution programs generally had more effect on recidivism than traditional probation, but not all restitution programs suppressed offense rates and not all outperformed the program against which they were compared. Traditional probation fared the worst in the analysis, as it seldom demonstrated even a reduction in postprogram offense rates and never produced better results than the restitution programs. Incarceration produced mixed results. The Boise short-term detention program was as effective as restitution, but the Ventura secure facility program was markedly less successful in suppressing offense rates than the residential work-release restitution program against which it was compared. Why do programs differ? Even more intriguing, why does the same type of program have different results in different places? In this chapter, the linkage mechanisms through which programs impact recidivism will be explored.

Programs and Perceptions

Restitution vs. Incarceration

Incarcerated juveniles, when compared with those who were randomly assigned into restitution, were more remorseful, believed their sanctions were less fair, were more certain of being caught, but paradoxically rated the expected punishment as less severe than did the restitution youths (see Table 7.1). Virtually all of the juveniles in both groups believed they would be incarcerated if they reoffended. Thus, the difference in their perception of the severity reflects different ratings of how much they dislike incarceration. Those who had actually experienced incarceration gave it a lower score than those who had not, implying that fear of incarceration diminishes once it is experienced. Juveniles in restitution programs in Boise had more positive citizenship images than those who had been incarcerated, but this relationship was not found in Ventura. As

TABLE 7.1. Program Effects on Perceptions, School, and Jobs (Zero Order Correlations).

	CITIZEN	REMORSE	FAIR	CERTAIN	SEVERE	INTENT	SCHOOL	JOB	SUCCESS
ALL CASES									
RESTN1	.00	−.08*	.04+	−.09*	.02	.05	−.01	.19*	.07*
RESINC	.03	−.16*	.14*	−.15*	.08	.17*	−.05	.09+	NA
RESPRO	−.03	−.03	.01	.00	.05	.02	.00	.15*	.00
RESAD	−.03	−.09	.10*	−.11*	.02	−.03	.03	.11*	.44
LPRIOR	−.09*	.01	−.05+	.04	.07*		−.15*	.00	.23*
INSUBS	−.13*	.02	−.03	.02	.09*		−.08	.00	.21*
SITES									
RESINC									
Ventra	−.18	−.15	.12	−.42	.18		.06	−.13	
Boise	.12┐	−.12┐	.17*	.03	.08	.07	−.02	−.04	
RESPRO									
Claytn	−.00	−.10+	−.17*	−.07	.06	.02	−.00	.07	.20*
Okla	−.03	.09	.14+	.14+	−.04	.02	−.08	.04	−.03
D.C.	−.12	−.04	.17*	.04	.05	.00	.10+	.29*	−.11
RESAD									
Ventra	−.14	−.10	.16+	−.14	−.06	.03	.14	.08	.16+
Dane	.02	−.08	.07	−.09	.04	.02	.00	.14*	.50*
PRIORS									
Vent	−.08	.01	−.01	−.12+	.17*		−.10*	−.03	
D.C.	−.20*	.08	−.06	.03	.05		−.19*	.01	
Claytn	−.11+	.00	−.03	.11+	.18*		−.23*	.11+	
Boise	.07	.03	−.12┐	.06	.09		−.24*	.20*	
Okla	−.07	.00	−.23*	−.04	.03		−.15+	−.23*	
Dane	−.00	−.03	.07	.06	−.00		−.05	−.05	
INSUBS									
Ventr	.03	−.07	.03	−.11	.15*		−.04	−.04	
D.C.	.04	.03	−.04	.07	.15*		−.04	−.04	
Clayt	−.27*	.13*	.00	.08	.09+		−.13*	.04	
Boise	−.29*	.02	−.28*	.02	.17┐		−.08	.05	
Okla	−.18*	−.07	−.27*	.07	−.09		.02	.00	
Dane	−.09+	−.09+	−.00	.03	.12*		.03	−.12*	

Figures are the zero order correlations between the variables shown on the left and those across the top. Juveniles were randomly assigned into restitution vs. incarceration, restitution vs. probation, and restitution vs. ad hoc restitution.

might be expected, juveniles in restitution programs had more jobs and were less likely to be in school.

Very few consistent differences were found between restitution and probation (except that restitution juveniles had held more jobs), but there were several site-specific effects that have important implications. In Clayton County, juveniles in restitution programs were less remorseful and believed their sanctions were less fair. In Oklahoma County, the juveniles believed their sanctions were more fair than those on probation and the restitution youth were more certain of being caught. In Washington, D.C., the restitution youth had a less positive self-image, but believed their sanctions were more fair. Within this group of comparisons, site-specific implementation and operation of the program had a more important impact on juvenile attitudes than did the underlying theory or philosophy of the program itself.

Comparisons between programmatic restitution and ad hoc restitution reveal some of the same patterns observed before: juveniles in restitution programs were less remorseful (although this difference was not statistically significant), believed their sanctions were more fair, and were less likely to believe they would be caught if they committed another offense. Those in programmatic restitution programs also had had more job experiences. Within this group, a strong relationship was found between programmatic restitution and successful completion of the program ($r = .44$).

In the lower portion of Table 7.1 are the zero order correlations between prior offenses, in-program offenses, and perceptions. Those who were committing more offenses during their time under the jurisdiction of the program had less positive images of themselves and were more inclined to define themselves as "lawbreakers" than were the other juveniles. Also, those who were committing more offenses believed they would be more severely punished if they were caught. It is interesting, however, that neither priors nor in-program offenses influenced the certainty of being caught. One of the most dramatic effects of prior delinquent behavior was on school status; in virtually every site those with prior offenses were less likely to be in school or to have graduated.

Discussion

There are several important findings here. Program effects on good citizen self-image varied from site to site and were governed mainly by site-specific implementation and practices rather than by the internal theory of the program itself. Sense of citizenship, for example, was enhanced by the restitution program in Boise, compared with the Boise detention program, but this pattern was not observed in any other place. In fact, the citizenship self-image was not strongly impacted by type of program at all, suggesting that this aspect of self-image may be more enduring and impervious to court interventions than might have been suspected.

One of the most intriguing findings is that the restitution experience often was associated with less remorseful juveniles than either incarceration or traditional probation. Restitution was associated with less remorse in Ventura, Boise, and Clayton County. It is possible that the restitution program emphasis on accountability may contribute to this effect. Many restitution programs, in an effort to avoid stigmitizing and labeling the youths, focus mainly on the offense and the youth's responsibility to make amends for the crime. There is less attention on their attitudes and on whether they accept responsibility for the crime, are sorry for it, believe that the victim did not deserve what happened to them, and so forth.

In several of the comparisons, juveniles in the restitution programs believed their sanctions were more fair than the control groups. Restitution was associated with a greater sense of fairness in Ventura (both groups), Boise, Oklahoma County, and Washington, D.C., but the restitution youth in Clayton viewed their sanction as less fair then those in probation. Why? Although there is no simple way to answer the question, the answer must lie in site-specific program characteristics. Another interesting finding is that youths in the traditional programs gave higher estimates of their likelihood of being caught and referred to court for subsequent offenses. The only exception was in Oklahoma County, which had a surprisingly high estimate of the likelihood of being caught (0.80 for both groups). Equally intriguing and counterintutive was the finding that juveniles who had experienced incarceration gave it a lower "dislike" score than those who had not experienced it.

Linking Program Experiences with Recidivism

A Methodological Note

The process model tested in this research links the type of program to success in the program and to the number of offenses committed while under program jurisdiction. These three variables are expected to influence perceptions of certainty, severity, citizenship, remorse, and fairness. Program experiences and perceptions are expected to be related to intentions of committing subsequent offenses as well as to the actual recontacts with the juvenile or adult court during the two- or three-year period after the youths left the program. Since perceptions were measured at the time the juveniles left the program, the temporal sequence of the data is consistent with the causal model. The number of jobs held by the juveniles and their school status also were incorporated as linkage variables. Prior offenses, age, race, and sex are used as control variables in testing the models.

Program success was measured in terms of compliance with program requirements, such as paying restitution or observing the rules of proba-

TABLE 7.2. Restitution vs. Incarceration in Boise Idaho: Multivariate Model.

N = 105	SUBS	INTENT	CITIZEN	REMORSE	FAIR	CERTAIN	SEVERE	INSUB	JOBS	SCHOOL
Resinc			.13	[.12]	.14			[−.09]		
Intent	.14									
Citizen	−.16	−.34								
Remorse	−.21	−.33								
Fair										
Certain										
Severe										
Priors		.15							.13	
Insub	.30		−.25		−.27					
Job		−.18	−.14		−.16					
School			.17							
Celerity										
Age			.41				−.21		.29	−.40
Minority									−.12	−.15
Male		−.15	.14						−.16	
R2	.20	.23	.19	.05	.08		.03		.10	.22

Cases for this analysis were from the Boise, Idaho experiment. N = 105. Values shown are the standardized regression coefficients, with the other variables controlled. All coefficients shown have an observed significance level of .05 or below, one-tailed tests, except those designated ⌉, which have an observed significance level between .05 and .10. Those shown in brackets have an o.s.l. between .10 and .20) The variable RESINC is a dummy coded variable representing the program effects, with restitution coded "1" and incarceration coded "0".

tion. Offenses committed while in the program were not used as an indicator of program failure. The number of in-program offenses refers to the actual count of offenses for which the youth was referred to court during the time he or she was in the program. Status offenses and technical violations of probation were not included. The recidivism variable LOUTSUB1 is the natural logarithim of the number of subsequent offenses committed after exiting the program, corrected for risk time. Each model is tested within the three contrasts permitted by the random assignment: restitution versus incarceration, restitution versus probation, and restitution versus ad hoc restitution. In each instance, restitution is coded "1" and the control condition is coded "0." Dummy variables representing each experiment in each site are included as controls to adjust for differences in means across sites and across different experiments within a particular site.

Restitution vs. Incarceration

The random assignment experiment in Boise, Idaho, produced the best data for comparing incarceration with restitution. As shown in Table 7.2 and Figure 7.1, the best predictors of recidivism for the Boise juveniles were the number of in-program offenses ($b = 0.30$), feelings of remorse ($b = -0.21$), intentions to commit crimes ($b = 0.14$), and sense of citizenship ($b = -0.16$). Persons who believed their sanctions were more fair also had lower recidivism rates ($r = -0.14$), but this relationship was reduced substantially when the remorse and citizenship variables were in the equation. Program effects were channeled through the citizenship variable ($b = 0.13$), the sense of remorse ($b = 0.12$), and through a reduction of in-program offending. Persons in restitution programs had a stronger sense of citizenship than those who were incarcerated, whereas those who were incarcerated had a greater sense of remorse than those in the restitution program.

FIGURE 7.1. Linkage Model: Restitution vs. Incarceration. (To avoid cluttering the diagram, not all variables are shown.)

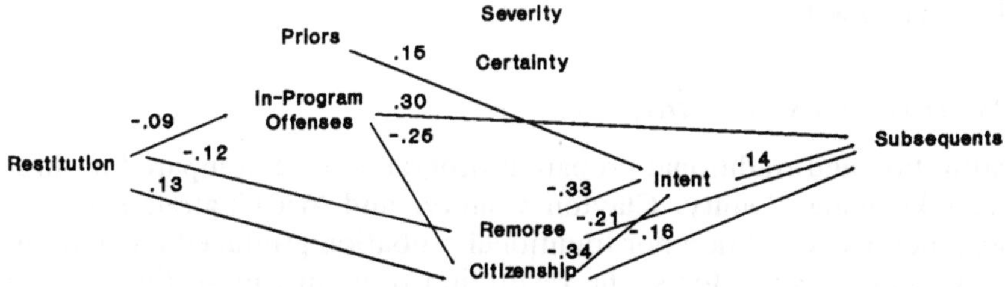

The results from the Ventura experiment were similar, although the small number of cases (35) precludes sophisticated analysis. In Ventura, the only substantial predictor of subsequent offenses was remorse ($b = -0.50$), and program type was the only predictor of remorse, with those who were incarcerated being more remorseful than those who were in the restitution program.

The pattern observed in Boise might be called an "offsetting" pattern in that experiences in restitution programs apparently increased the sense of citizenship more so than experiences in incarceration, but decreased the sense of remorse. Incarceration, then, was associated with a more negative citizenship self image, but with greater remorse. Since both citizenship and remorse depressed recidivism, the effects are offsetting, and there was no net advantage for either restitution or incarceration on recidivism. The restitution program also was slightly more effective in reducing the rate of in-program offending ($b = -0.09$) which had a strong effect on the rate of postprogram offending ($b = 0.30$).

It should be recalled from Chapter 6 that both the restitution program and the detention program in Boise had suppressant effects on offense rates. The interesting possibility is that the detention program relied heavily on inculcating the youths with feelings of remorse for what they did, whereas the restitution program relied more on strengthening self-image as a positive, law-abiding citizen. And, both may owe their success to the particular strategy they adopted. In fact, it is possible that the program philosophy and strategy influence the predictors of recidivism for the juveniles under its jurisdiction. This possibility will be explored later.

The deterrence model received almost no support in the Boise experiment. Incarcerated youth were no more certain they would be caught in the future than were the juveniles in the restitution programs. The youth who were incarcerated rated the severity of their punishment at about the same level as the juveniles in the restitution program. Even more damaging to the deterrence model is the fact that perceptions of certainty and severity were irrelevant to the rate of subsequent offending. The ability of incarceration to reduce recidivism appears to lie in its effect on remorse, not in its ability to frighten juveniles into avoiding crime. Its weakness is its association with the juveniles' sense that they are lawbreakers rather than good citizens.

Restitution vs. Probation

Restititution and traditional probation programs were compared in three sites: Oklahoma County, Clayton County, and Washington, D.C. Although neither restitution nor traditional probation produced much in the way of suppression effects, the restitution programs in all three places had lower postprogram offense rates. The multivariate linkage model (see Table 7.3 and Figure 7.2) shows that the most important predictors of recidivism were prior offenses ($b = 0.02$), in-program offenses ($b = .10$), certainty of punishment ($b = 0.10$), citizenship ($b = -.09$), fewer jobs ($b = .09$), and intent ($b = .07$). Within this group, persons who were more certain they would be caught committed more offenses, rather than fewer, thereby reversing the relationship expected by deterrence theory. It has already been pointed out, however, that the measure of certainty taken at the time of the interview relates in the expected way to intentions to commit crimes. The logical explanation is that perceptions of certainty are highly specific to the context and can be expected to change dramatically once a particular crime opportunity is being considered.

The comparative advantage of the restitution program in reducing recidivism when compared with traditional probation appears to lie in its ability to suppress the rate of offending when the youth is under program jurisdiction and in its higher rate of successful completion. Restitution had a higher probability of successful completion than did probation and successful completion was related to less in program offending. Restitution had an independent effect in reducing in-program offending as well. The reduction in in-program offenses was directly related to a reduction in postprogram recidivism and to an enhanced sense of citizenship that, in turn, was associated with lower delinquency rates after the youth left the program.

Perceptions of certainty and severity were related in the expected way to intentions of reoffending, but not to actual recontact with the court. As expected, there were no differences between restitution and probation groups in their perceptions of certainty or severity.

The models within Clayton County and Oklahoma County both resemble the one shown for the pooled data. In Clayton County, the best predictors of subsequents were citizenship ($b = -0.13$), priors ($b = 0.19$), and in-program offenses ($b = 0.13$). Persons in the restitution program had a higher rate of success, which was related to lower in-program subsequents. Restitution also had a small direct effect ($b = -0.08$) on in-program subsequents. The model in Oklahoma County was similar, in that in-program subsequents were the best predictor of postprogram offenses and program success was the best predictor of in-program offenses. But the restitution program in Oklahoma County did not produce higher success rates than the probation program. However, it showed an independent effect on in-program subsequents of about the same size observed in the other sites ($b = -0.09$).

The pattern that emerged from the restitution probation comparisons may be a developmental one in which initial program successes and other program efforts reduce in-program offending, breaking the pattern of behavior and contributing directly to reduced recidivism. Program success

TABLE 7.3. Restitution vs. Probation: Multivariate Model.

N=409	SUBS	INTENT	CITIZEN	REMORSE	FAIR	CERTAIN	SEVERE	INSUB	JOBS	SCHOOL	SUCCESS
ResPro								−.09	.14		
Success			.18		.15			−.12			
Intent	.07										
Citizen	−.09	.22									
Remorse											
Fair											
Certain	.10	−.13									
Severe		−.09									
Priors	.20		−.10				.10	.22		−.16	−.11
Insub	.10		−.13	.07							
Job	.09										
School	−.09										.09
Age	−.18		.17						.34	−.29	
Minority				−.19					−.20		−.20
Female		−.10	.10					−.07	−.12		
R2	.12	.08	.10	.01	.02	.13	.01	.09	.32	.13	.06

Values shown are the standardized regression coefficients, with the other variables controlled. All coefficients shown have an observed significance level of .05 or below, one-tailed tests, except those designated ¬, which have an observed significance level between .05 and .10. Dummy variables for the sites were included in the analysis as controls to adjust for differences across the courts represented in this analysis. The variable RESPRO is a dummy coded variable representing the program effects, with restitution coded "1" and probation coded "0".

FIGURE 7.2. Linkage Model: Restitution vs. Probation. (To avoid cluttering the diagram, not all linkages are shown.)

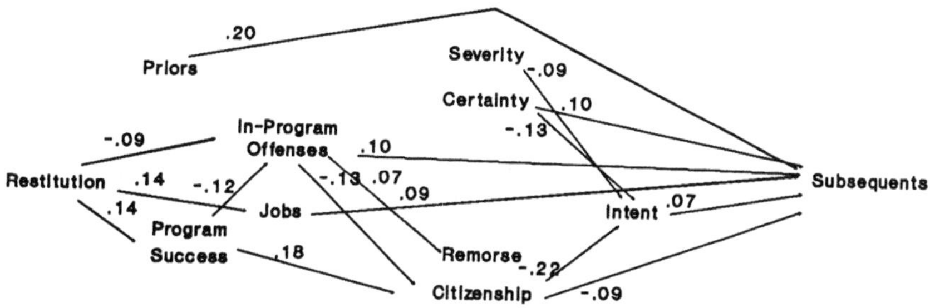

contributes to the sense of citizenship, which in turn reduces subsequents.

Programmatic Restitution vs. Ad Hoc Restitution

The developmental model involving successful completion of the program and a heightened sense of citizenship was even more apparent in the comparison of programmatic restitution and ad hoc restitution (Table 7.4 and Figure 7.3). The main difference between these programs, as noted previously, was that the restitution programs viewed restitution as an integral part of the youth's rehabilitation plan—indeed, restitution was viewed as the most important requirement the court had made in the case. These programs had an identifiable staff and organization and were responsible for providing assistance to the juveniles in complying with the restitution and community service requirements. In the ad hoc approaches, the court-ordered restitution was handled by the county clerk's office and probation officers were scarcely aware of the orders and were not expected to implement or monitor them and restitution was not viewed as part of the overall treatment program for the youth. It is fair to say that the only difference between the ad hoc restitution programs and traditional probation was that the court had ordered restitution to be paid in the latter. It was left to the juvenile and his or her family to pay it.

The data in Chapter 6 showed that ad hoc and programmatic restitution both produced suppression effects but that the programmatic approaches had a more substantial impact on recidivism when postprogram rates were compared. Programmatic restitution could produce lower rates of recidivism than ad hoc approaches because program personnel did a better job inculcating the values associated with restitution, or because juveniles in the programmatic approaches were better able to be successful in completing their restitution, or both. Success in repaying victims may be

TABLE 7.4. Restitution vs. Ad Hoc Restitution: Multivariate Model.

N=363	SUBS	INTENT	CITIZEN	REMORSE	FAIR	CERTAIN	SEVERE	INSUB	JOB	SCHOOL	SUCCESS
ResAd			−.12	−.12	−.14	−.11			.10		.42
Success	−.14	−.13	.20		.14			−.31			
Intent											
Citizen	−.17	−.17									
Remorse											
Fair		−.14									
Certain		−.19									
Severe											
Priors	.27							.22		−.11	
Insub	.18						.13				
Job		−.11		.09							
School		−.09					−.09				
Age	−.11		−.10		−.13	−.17	−.14	−.09	−.19	−.20	.14
Minority	.15	−.11		−.15					−.16		−.16
Female					−.12						
R2	.26	.14	.03	.03	.05	.04	.08	.18	.10	.05	.23

Values shown are the standardized regression coefficients, with the other variables controlled. All coefficients shown have an observed significance level of .05 or below, one-tailed tests, except those designated ⌉, which have an observed significance level between .05 and .10. Dummy variables for the sites were included in the analysis as controls to adjust for differences across the courts represented in this analysis. The variable RESAD is a dummy coded variable representing the program effects, with programmatic restitution coded "1" and ad hoc approaches coded "0".

FIGURE 7.3. Linkage Model: Restitution vs. Ad Hoc Restitution. (To avoid cluttering the diagram, not all variables are shown.)

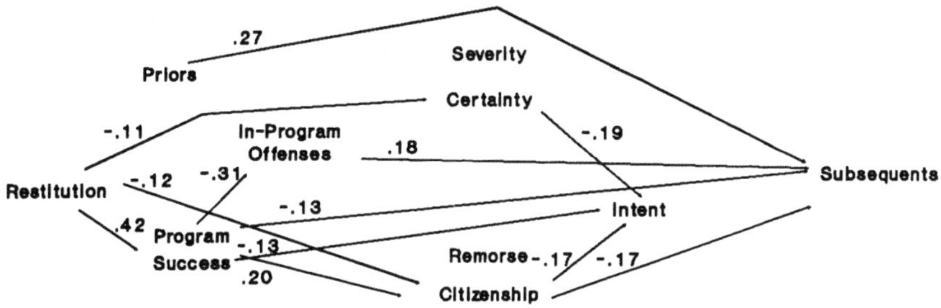

associated with a sense of accomplishment and with more positive self-image, which in turn are related to lower recidivism.

The results suggest that the comparative advantage for programmatic approaches lies principally in their ability to increase the proportion of juveniles who were able to complete their restitution requirements successfully. Programmatic approaches had a strong relationship to successful completion ($r = 0.42$), which was strongly associated with lower in-program offending ($b = -0.31$). Both of these variables had direct relationships to lower subsequents and program success also enhanced the sense of citizenship, which was also related to lower postprogram offenses.

Within the two sites that contributed cases to this anlysis (Dane and Ventura), the same patterns were found. The best predictors of subsequent offenses were in-program subsequents and the sense of citizenship, both of which were influenced strongly by program success. In both sites, the restitution cases had higher successful completion rates than cases in the ad hoc approaches.

The Pooled Data

When all the data were pooled, the final model shows both the offsetting and the developmental pattern (Table 7.5 and Figure 7.4). Program type was included as a dummy variable with restitution scored as "0" and all controls scored as "1." The best predictors of lower rates of postprogram offending were fewer priors, fewer in-program offenses, higher sense of citizenship, more remorse, less intent to reoffend, and higher rates of success in the program.

Program effects operated mainly through reduction in in-program offending and through the juvenile's ability to comply with programmatic requirements. Specifically, juveniles in restitution programs were less likely to commit crimes during their time in the program and juveniles who committed fewer crimes while they were under court supervision

TABLE 7.5. Program Type, Perceptions, and Recidivism: Multivariate Model for Pooled Sample.

N=857	SUBS	INTENT	CITIZEN	REMORSE	FAIR	CERTAIN	SEVERE	INSUB	JOB	SCHOOL	SUCCESS
Program				−.06	.05+		.05	−.07	.08		.10
Success	−.06	−.08	.12	−.07	.10			−.19			
Intent	.05										
Citizen	−.11	−.23									
Remorse	−.06+	−.06+									
Fair		−.06+									
Certain	.07	−.14									
Severe											
Priors	.17						.07	.21		−.12	−.09
Insub	.13		−.10				.08				.16
Job		−.07		−.07							.08
School	−.08	−.05	.08								.06
Age	−.14		.12			−.08	−.05		.25	−.29	.06
Minority	.14			−.22					−.17		−.23
Female	−.09	−.12						−.06	−.08		
R2	.15	.15	.14	.04	.05	.10	.08	.07	.37	.15	.14

Values shown are the standardized regression coefficients, with the other variables controlled. All coefficients shown have an observed significance level of .05 or below, one-tailed tests, except those designated ⌉, which have an observed significance level between .05 and .10. Dummy variables for the sites were included in the analysis as controls to adjust for differences across the courts represented in this analysis. The variable RESNI is a dummy coded variable representing the program effects, with programmatic restitution coded "1" and all other programs coded "0".

FIGURE 7.4. Linkage Model: All Cases. (To avoid cluttering the diagram, not all variables are shown.)

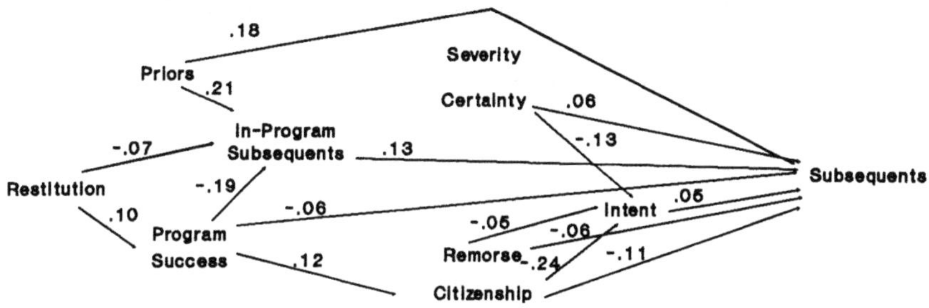

also committed fewer crimes after they were released. Furthermore, those who were able to remain relatively crime-free while in the program had stronger self-images (as good citizens, rather than lawbreakers) and had stronger intentions of remaining crime-free. Both of these variables were related to reduced recidivism. As revealed earlier, the effect of incarceration on recidivism was through heightened remorse, rather than through beliefs in the certainty or severity of punishment. Persons in restitution programs believed their sanctions were more fair, but fairness had only a very weak relationship (through intentions) to subsequent offenses. Certainty of punishment had a weak but statistically significant relationship opposite that expected by deterrence theory: those who were more certain they would be caught actually committed more offenses than those who were less certain they would be caught. Perceptions of punishment severity were not related to subsequent court contacts.

Discussion

The attempt to understand how and why juvenile justice programs influence recidivism has revealed a clear and interesting pattern. The programs studied here either had direct effects on sense of citizenship and remorse that were then related to postprogram offense rates or they had indirect effects through their ability to help juveniles achieve successful completion of the program requirements, or their ability to suppress the rate of in-program offending, or both. Successful completion and reduced rates of offending during the time in the program had direct effects on reduced recidivism and enhanced the sense of citizenship, which in turn influenced recidivism.

The major conclusions that can be drawn at this point are that normative perceptual models outperformed the deterrence models. Restitution programs were more likely to reduce recidivism than probation because they had higher rates of successful completion and lower in-program offense rates, and they enhanced the sense of citizenship. For these reasons, programmatic restitution outperformed ad hoc restitution. When restitution was compared with incarceration, offsetting effects seem to exist. The incarceration experience increases remorse, which is associated with lower recidivism; but restitution increases the sense of citizenship, which also lowers recidivism.

8 Conclusions

Modern American society is permeated by the belief that human beings are driven by self-interested behavior and that public policies can influence behavior by manipulating the costs, benefits, or risks of alternative actions. Simplified versions of expected utility theory hold that behavior is contingent upon net utility and that it does not matter much, if at all, whether one seeks to change behavior by altering the benefits, altering the costs, or reducing uncertainty. The modern revival of deterrence theory as a guide to criminal and juvenile justice policy rests precisely upon these contentions. Even if criminal behavior might be reduced substantially through changes in social institutions that provide greater opportunity for individuals, such changes are viewed as too indirect and expensive when compared against the simpler options of increasing the severity, celerity, or certainty of punishment. Even juvenile justice policy is becoming increasingly reliant on punishment or the threat of punishment to discourage criminal behavior and to change the lifestyles of convicted juvenile offenders.

Expected utility theory, including deterrence theory, has several drawbacks, however, as a guide to policy as well as a general theory of behavior. First, individuals make numerous errors in their estimates of benefits, costs, and risks, therefore making it very difficult for them to make decisions that will be consistent with objective estimates of net utility. Second, expected utility theory does not take into account the predecision processes through which individuals frame situations, seek ideas, and devise courses of actions. Third, even when persons are directly confronted with choices and relatively clear information, they usually do not choose options on the basis of net utility, particularly under conditions of uncertainty. Instead, most rely on decision heuristics, short cuts, or rules of thumb, that are used in lieu of calculations about the future consequences of various alternatives.

Even as policy makers seem intent on applying the principles of expected utility theory generally, and deterrence specifically, social and behavioral scientists are developing more complex theories of decision and behavior—theories that are more firmly grounded in empirical research. This research repeatedly finds that norms, values, experiences, opportunities, and pure happenstance are important in understanding how choices emerge. Decisions and actions under conditions of uncertainty depend heavily on the circumstances leading up to the decision situation as well as on how the situation is framed and where (or whether) the person searches for information. These processes, in turn, are guided more by decision heuristics than by rational calculation of future expected outcomes.

The research reported here compares the effects of alternative juvenile justice policies on subsequent criminal behavior and seeks to identify the perceptual linkages through which public policies influence juveniles to change their behavior. Drawing upon results from six random-assignment experiments conducted in six different United States cities, the findings have implications for public policy, decision theory, and future public policy research.

Program Effects on Recidivism

Three of the most common dispositional alternatives available to juvenile courts—restitution, probation, and incarceration—were compared in the six random-assignment experiments. The restitution programs were programmatic approaches with identifiable staff and a guiding philosophy that juveniles should be held accountable to victims and community for their offenses, but in a nonpunitive, positive manner that would permit the offender to regain self-respect as well as permit the victim to be paid reparations. From this perspective, juvenile offenders were not to be treated as persons suffering from fundamental character defects but as persons who made mistakes that should be rectified and not repeated. In the restitution programs, juveniles were required to pay monetary restitution or perform community service work to repay the victims. Staff were responsible for developing the restitution plan, assisting the juveniles in locating paid or volunteer work, monitoring work performance through contacts with employers, and closing the cases when the juveniles had finished paying the victims. These juveniles were on probation, but the probationary requirements focused extensively or exclusively on restitution, rather than the more common counseling approaches. The incarceration programs included a short-term detention program in Boise, Idaho, where the juveniles were detained for several weekends and remained on probation for one year. In Ventura, California, the incarceration program was a more traditional institutional setting.

Focusing first on suppression effects, where the preintervention and postintervention annual offense rates were compared, the analysis revealed that restitution and detention both had suppression effects but probation did not. More specifically:

1. Restitution programs—8 tests, 6 showed suppression effects, 2 did not.
2. Detention—1 test (Boise) showed suppression effects.
3. Probation—3 tests, 1 showed suppression effects, 2 did not.
4. Ad hoc (nonprogrammatic) restitution programs—2 tests, 1 showed suppression effects, 1 did not.

Although suppression effects are interesting because they imply that policy interventions slow or halt the rate of offending, there are methodological problems in separating the true effect of the programs from other factors.

The experimental nature of the research, relying upon random assignment between restitution and the other dispositions, permits a more reliable test of the impact of each disposition on recidivism. These results generally favored the restitution programs over probation and showed no discernable differences between restitution and incarceration. (There were no direct comparisons of probation with incarceration.) Specifically, the results indicate that restitution programs produced a higher percentage of juveniles who ceased their delinquent activity during the two- or three-year followup (57% reoffending, compared with 64% for the other dispositions); and produced a lower annual offense rate (0.64 per youth per year, compared with 0.80 per youth per year for the traditional dispositions).

Other results mirrored the findings from the analysis of suppression effects: restitution programs were more effective than probation, had the same level of effectiveness as detention, and the programmatic approaches to restitution were far more effective than the ad hoc approaches. When the results were analyzed in a multivariate framework to hold constant other variables and to reduce some of the problems introduced by a less than perfect adherence to random assignment, the results were essentially unchanged. Restitution was more effective than probation; there was a short-term advantage to restitution over detention but the overall effect including the two years of followup showed no significant differences; and the programmatic approaches were more effective than the ad hoc programs. All these differences were statistically significant at 0.05 or beyond.

As a general conclusion, it appears that the restitution programs usually reduced recidivism (although this was not true in all programs); and never had a negative effect or an effect that was less pronounced than the dispositional alternative against which it was compared. Overall, the restitution programs produced an estimated decline of 18 offenses per year for every 100 juveniles. The average loss for the juvenile crimes included in this study was slightly over $600. Thus, a decline of 18 offenses per year is far from a trivial effect, as a normal city of a half million persons can expect 10,000 or more juvenile referrals each year.

The comparison of different programs in six different cities also revealed that several different kinds of juvenile programs may have positive effects and that the underlying program theory is not the only important variable. A great deal depends upon the implementation of the program and the skills of the staff. Nevertheless, the results suggest that restitution programs may be somewhat more robust than other types and may be more effective under a variety of different conditions. Still, the implementation and operation of specific programs are extremely important and one cannot expect programs of a particular type to always outperform other kinds of programs.

Effect of Perceptions on Recidivism

Why and how do programs produce effects on behavior? Decision theory holds that environmental stimuli—ranging from intervention programs to basic socioeconomic environmental conditions—influence behavior only by influencing perceptions or beliefs such as norms; attitudes; self-image; beliefs about the certainty, severity, or celerity of punishment; and so forth. Decision heuristics theory argues that linkages to behavior should be examined from an empirical basis and the specific attitudes or perceptions that are important in governing behavior should be established empirically.

The decision model examined in this research focused first on self-reported intentions of committing subsequent crimes and then on actual recidivism rates during the two- or three-year followup period. Intentions to commit crimes were included because these imply a commitment to avoid (or not avoid) future criminal activity and because they permit a more direct test of the coherence of individual belief systems. Variables tested for their importance in understanding intentions and actual recidivism included perceptions of certainty and severity of punishment, self-image as a good citizen rather than as a lawbreaker, remorse for the crime that had been committed, and perceptions of the fairness of the sanction itself. Several other variables were examined but discarded as they were not important, including empathy for the victim.

Analysis of intentions to avoid crime revealed that even though perceptions of certainty and severity were important, the best predictor of intentions was self-image as a good citizen, followed by the degree of remorse. Beliefs that the sanctions were fair also were related to lower intentions of reoffending. Sense of citizenship was related to lower intentions of reoffending in all six sites, and was statistically significant beyond 0.001 in all six.

Analysis of actual recontact with the juvenile or adult court during the two- or three-year followup period, however, revealed a markedly different pattern for the deterrence variables of certainty and severity. Persons who believed they were more likely to be caught actually committed more subsequent offenses, rather than fewer, and those who believed they would be punished more severely also committed more, rather than fewer, offenses. On the other hand, the sense of citizenship and sense of remorse were related as expected to lower recidivism rates. Juveniles with a self-image as a good citizen were considerably less likely to recidivate, as were those who were more remorseful.

Why do juveniles who think they will be caught and who believe they will be punished severely commit more offenses? A host of methodological explanations were examined and all were rejected. Analyses were conducted to determine whether severity of punishment would be important if certainty was high enough; this was rejected. Another analysis examined whether certainty would be important for persons who believed they would be punished severely. This, too, was rejected. A proposition that certainty and severity would be important at first but the effects would decay over time was examined and found not to be important. A macho explanation was attempted, in which juveniles who enjoyed crime (i.e., viewed it as "fun," "exciting," "dangerous," and so forth) would overestimate certainty and severity of punishment, thereby masking the true relationship between the deterrence variables and recidivism. There was no support for this contention in the data, either. A proposition that certainty and severity of punishment would become important for especially high rate offenders was partially supported, as perceptions of severity of punishment were related to lower offending for persons with six or more prior offenses. This suggests that there may be a point in a juvenile career where some of the youths recognize the severity of future actions and intentionally reduce or cease their criminal activity. Most juveniles, however, do not seem to reduce their criminal activity as a result of perceived certainty and severity.

There are several plausible explanations. One is that juveniles who are committing crimes and engaging in a criminal lifestyle at the time of the interview and those who fully intend to continue committing crimes KNOW they will be caught, and they KNOW they will be punished severely. In other words, high rate offenders are simply realistic about their prospects of capture and punishment. Unfortunately for advocates of deterrence and punishment, however, these perceptions do not translate into reduced offending. Another plausible explanation is that perceptions of certainty are highly contingent upon context and there is no generalized sense of the certainty of arrest. Thus, a person's perception of certainty will vary dramatically depending upon the context; the certainty of capture that is relevant for offending is that which stems from the actual crime situation that is being contemplated. Assessments of punishment severity may follow the same pattern. Offenses may not begin with the intent to commit a particularly serious crime, hence the perception of severity is underestimated.

In contrast with the deterrence variables, a sense of citizenship and remorse was an important variable in understanding recidivism. The findings provide far more support to decision heuristic theories that emphasize the importance of basic values and self-image than to deterrence theories that focus on perceptions of certainty and severity of punishment. The data suggest that normative and ethical considerations guide the manner in which individuals frame situations and influence the nature of alternatives that are taken into consideration. Crime opportunities are everywhere; they present themselves on a regular and recurring basis to every citizen. Persons who view themselves as honest, law-abiding, citizens may not even recognize these opportunities, much less seek them out. And people who view themselves as good citizens often forego engaging in criminal opportunities, even when the chances are quite remote of being captured. Normative orientations and self-image provide a simple rule of behavior. People know what kind of person they are and they usually make decisions and engage in behavior consistent with that image.

Program Interventions, Perceptions, and Results

The final linkage in the decision model involves the translation of experiences in the juvenile justice system into behavioral results, and the mechanisms through which different types of programs produce different types of effects. This analysis revealed two distinct patterns: an "offsetting" pattern and a "developmental" pattern.

Comparisons of restitution programs with detention and incarceration indicate the possibility that experiences in restitution programs enhance the sense of citizenship, whereas experiences in detention either have no effect or damage citizenship. In contrast, however, experiences in restitution either have no effect on remorse or reduce remorse, whereas experiences in detention or incarceration increase the extent of remorse. Both restitution and detention have suppression effects. Thus, there is an interesting possibility that these programs work through different mechanisms in reducing recidivism: restitution working through enhanced sense of citizenship and detention working through increased remorse. One of the interesting implications here is that punishment policies such as detention or incarceration (which incidentally were viewed as much more severe than restitution by the juveniles) do not operate on recidivism through changes in perceptions of certainty and severity but through remorse. Further, if these programs could avoid damaging an individual's sense that he or she is a good, honest, law-abiding citizen the programs would be more effective. For restitution programs, the implication is that if they could increase the juvenile's sense of remorse without damaging self-image, then they too might be more effective.

Comparisons of restitution and probation suggest that restitution is more effective in reducing recidivism because it provides the juveniles with immediate and continuing success in the program. In other words, the juveniles can quickly develop a sense of being successful by obtaining employment and beginning to make their restitution payments or perform their community service work. The data suggest that this reduces the offense activity during the time they are in the program. The sense of success and the reduced in-program offense rate both enhance the juvenile's sense of citizenship as well as reduced intentions to reoffend and actual recontacts with the court.

Comparisons of the programmatic approaches to restitution with the ad hoc or insurance approaches in which the judge orders restitution, but the youth is simply left to his or her own devices to pay, show a clear superiority for the former. The analysis indicates that the main problems with the ad hoc approaches are the same as found with the traditional probation programs. There are no clear or tangible actions for which the youth can feel a sense of accomplishment and success. In-program offense rates do not decline as much for the ad hoc approaches and the sense of citizenship is not as high. These variables, in turn, have effects on recidivism.

There are a number of policy and theoretical implications of the study reported here. Punishment policies, such as detention or incarceration, are no more effective than restitution programs, although the data suggest that program implementation and staff skills are important factors regardless of the underlying theory of the policy intervention. Restitution programs, if approached from a programmatic perspective, are more effective than traditional probation. Restitution without a programmatic approach, however, is considerably less effective than programmatic restitution. Although much more research needs to be undertaken to understand the linkages between experiences, perceptions, and recidivism, the data here suggest that programs will be more effective if they can provide a more tangible measure of success for the juvenile, reduce the rate of in-program offending, increase remorse, and simultaneously enhance the juvenile's sense of citizenship.

From the perspective of theory, the research suggests the importance of decision heuristics and the importance of continuing to search for perceptual linkages between experiences and future behavior. Continued reliance on overly simplistic notions of expected utility theory, particularly under conditions of uncertainty, is not likely to produce better theory or improved public policy. Norms, values, self-image, context, and pure happenstance are important in understanding the linkage between policy and behavior.

References

Arrow, K.J. (1983). Gifts and exchanges. In E. Phelps (Ed.), *Altruism, morality and economic theory* (pp. 13–28). New York: Russell Sage Foundation.

Axelrod, R. (1980). An evolutionary approach to norms. *American Political Science Review, 80,* 1095–1112.

Bailey, W.C. (1976). Certainty of arrest and crime rates for major felonies. *Journal of Research in Crime and Delinquency,* July, 145–153.

Becker, G. (1968). Crime and punishment: An economic approach. *Journal of Political Economy, 76,* 169–217.

Bishop, D.M. (1984). Legal and extralegal barriers to delinquency. *Criminology, 22,* 403–419.

Block, M.K., & Heineke, J.M. (1975). A labor theoretic analysis of the criminal choice. *American Economic Review, 65,* 314–325.

Block, M.K., & Lind, R. (1975). An economic analysis of crimes punishable by imprisonment. *Journal of Legal Studies, 4,* 479–492.

Blumstein, A., Cohen, J., & Nagin, D. (Eds.) (1978). *Deterrence and incapacitation: Estimating the effects of criminal sanctions on crime rates.* Washington, D.C.: National Academy of Sciences.

Blumstein, A., Cohen, J., & Farrington, D.P. (1988). Criminal career research: Its value for criminology. *Criminology, 26,* (1) Feb., 1–35.

Blumstein, A., Cohen, J., & Farrington, D.P. (1988). Longitudinal and criminal career research: Further clarifications. *Criminology, 26,* (1) Feb., 57–74.

Bonta, J.L., Boyl, J., Motiuk, L.L., & Sonnichsen, P. (1983). Restitution in correctional half-way houses: Victim satisfaction, attitudes and recidivism. *Canadian Journal of Corrections, 20,* 140–152.

Bridges, G., & Stone, J.A., (1986). Effects of criminal punishment on perceived threat of punishment: Toward an understanding of specific deterrence. *Journal of Research in Crime and Delinquency, 23,* 207–239.

Brown, D., & McDougal, S.L. (1978). Noncompliance with law: A utility analysis of city crime rates. *Social Science Quarterly, 59,* 195–214.

Cannon, A., & Stanford, R.M. (1981). *Evaluation of the juvenile alternative services project.* Unpublished. Florida Department of Health and Rehabilitative Services.

Carroll, J.S. (1978). A psychological approach to deterrence: The evaluation of crime opportunities. *Journal of Personality and Social Psychology, 36,* 1512–1520.

Carroll, J., & Weaver, F. (1986). Shoplifters' perceptions of crime opportunities: A process-tracing study. In D.B. Cornish & R.V. Clarke, *The reasoning criminal* (pp. 19–31). New York: Springer-Verlag.

Cohen, L., & Stark, R. (1974). Discriminatory labeling and the five-finger discount. *Journal of Research in Crime and Delinquency, 11,* 25–39.

Cook, P.J. (1986). Criminal incapacitation effects considered in an adaptive choice framework. In D.B. Cornish & R.V. Clarke (Eds.), *The reasoning criminal* (pp. 202–213). New York: Springer-Verlag.

Cook, P.J. (1980). Research in criminal deterrence: Laying the groundwork for the second decade. In N. Morris & M. Tonry (Eds.), *Crime and justice: An annual review of research.* Chicago, Ill.: The University of Chicago Press.

Cook, T. (1985). Postpositivist critical multiplism. In R.L. Shotland & M. M. Mard (Eds.) *Social science and social policy.* Beverly Hills: Sage.

Cornish, D.B., & R.V. Clarke, (1986). *The reasoning criminal.* New York: Springer-Verlag.

Cullen, F.T., & Gendreau, P. (1989). The effectiveness of correctional rehabilitation: Reconsidering the "nothing works" debate. In L. Goodstein & D. Mackenzie (Eds.), *The American prison: Issues in research and policy.* New York: Plenum.

Currie, E. (1985). *Confronting crime.* New York: Pantheon Books.

Deutsch, M. (1985). *Distributive justice.* New Haven, Conn.: Yale University Press.

Deutsch, S.J., & Alt, F.B. (1977). The effect of Massachusetts' gun control law on gun-related crimes in the city of Boston. *Evaluation Quarterly, 1,* 543–568.

Eckland-Olson, S., Lieb, J., & Zurcher, L. (1984). The paradoxical impact of criminal sanctions: Some microstructural findings. *Law and Society Review, 28,* 159–178.

Edwards, W. (1955). The prediction of decision among bets. *Journal of Experimental Psychology, 50,* 201–214.

Ehrlich, I. (1975). The deterrent effect of capital punishment: A question of life and death. *American Economic Review, 65,* 397–417.

Ehrlich, I. (1973). Participation in illegitimate activities: A theoretical and empirical investigation. *Journal of Political Economy, 81,* 521–565.

Elliott, D.S. & Ageton, S. (1980). Reconciling race and class differences in self-reported and official estimates of delinquency. *American Sociological Review, 45,* 95–110.

Elliott, D.S., & Huizinga, D. (1983). Social class and delinquent behavior in a

Elliott, D.S., & Huizinga, D. (1983). Social class and delinquent behavior in a national youth panel. *Criminology, 2,* May, 149–177.

Empey, L. (1982). *American delinquency.* Homewood, Ill.: The Dorsey Press.

Erickson, M., & Gibbs, J.P. (1979). On the perceived severity of legal penalties. *Journal of Criminal Law and Criminology, 70,* 102–116.

Erickson, M., Gibbs, J.P., & Jensen, G.F. (1977). The deterrence doctrine and the perceived certainty of legal punishments. *American Sociological Review, 43,* April, 305–317.

Fattah, E.A. (1983). A critique of deterrence research with particular reference to the economic approach. *Canadian Journal of Criminology,* 79–90.

Feeney, F. (1986). Robbers as decision makers. In D.B. Cornish & R.V. Clarke, *The reasoning criminal* (pp. 53–71). New York: Springer-Verlag.

Forst, B. (1976). Participation in illegitimate activities: Further empirical findings. *Policy Analysis, 2,* 477–492.

Garrett, C.J. (1985). Effects of residential treatment on adjudicated delinquents: A meta analysis. *Journal of Research in Crime and Delinquency, 22,* 287–308.

Geerken, M.R., & Gove, W.R. (1975). Deterrence: Some theoretical considerations. *Law and Society Review, 9,* 497–513.

Geerken, M.R., & Gove, W.R. (1977). Deterrence, overload, and incapacitation: An empirical evaluation. *Social Forces, 56,* (2), 425–447.

Gendreau, P., & Ross, R.R. (1981). Correctional potency: Treatment and deterrence on trial. In R. Roesch and R.R. Coprrado (Eds.), *Evaluation and Criminal Justice Policy* (pp. 30–57). Beverly Hills: Sage.

Gendreau, P., & Ross, R.R. (1987). Revivification of rehabilitation: Evidence from the 1980s. *Justice Quarterly, 4,* 349–407.

Gibbs, J.P. (1977). Social control, deterrence, and perspectives on social order. *Social Forces, 56,* 409–423.

Gold, M., & Williams, J. (1969). National study of the aftermath of apprehension. *Prospectus, 3,* 3–11.

Gottfredson, M. & Hirschi, T. (1988). Science, public policy, and the career paradigm. *Criminology,* 26 (1) Feb., 37–55.

Gove, W. (Ed.). (1980). *The Labelling of deviance.* Beverly Hills: Sage.

Grasmick, H.G. (1982). The strategy of deterrence research: A reply to Greenberg. *Journal of Criminal Law and Criminology, 72,* (3) 1102–1108.

Grasmick, H.G., & Appleton, L. (1977). Legal punishment and social stigma: A comparison of two deterrence models. *Social Science Quarterly, 58,* 15–28.

Grasmick, H.G., & Bryjak, G.J. (1980). The deterrent effect of perceived severity of punishment. *Social Forces, 59,* 471–491.

Grasmick, H.G., & Green, D.E. (1980). Legal punishment, social disapproval, and internalization as inhibitors of illegal behavior. *Journal of Criminal Law and Criminology, 71,* 325–335.

Green, G. (1985). General deterrence and television cable crime: A field experiment in social control. *Criminology, 23,* (4) 629–646.

Greenberg, D.F., & Kessler, R.C. (1982). The effect of arrests on crime: A multivariate panel analysis. *Social Forces, 60,* March, 771–790.

Greenberg, D. (1981) Methodological issues in survey research on the inhibition of crime. *Journal of Criminal Law and Criminology, 72,* (3) 1094–1101.

Griffith, W.R. (1983). *The self report instrument: A description and analysis of results in the national evaluation sites.* Eugene, Ore.: Institute of Policy Analysis.

Griffith, W. (1983). *The official records check: Preliminary response rates in the national evaluation sites.* Eugene, Ore.: Institute of Policy Analysis.

Guedalia, L.J. (1979). *Predicting recidivism of juvenile delinquents on restitutionary probation from selected background, subject, and program variables.* Unpublished doctoral dissertation. Washington, D.C.: American University.

Heinz, J., Galaway, B., & Hudson, J. (1976). Restitution or parole: A follow-up study of adult offenders. *Social Service Review, 50,* 148–156.

Heinz, A., Jaboc, H., & Lineberry, R.L. (1983). Crime in city politics. New York: Longman.

Hirschi, T. (1969). *Causes of delinquency.* Berkeley, Calif.: University of California Press.

Hirschi, T. (1986). On the compatibility of rational choice and social control theories of crime. In D.B. Cornish, & R.V. Clarke, *The reasoning criminal* (pp. 105–118). New York: Springer-Verlag.

Hofford, M. (1981). *Juvenile restitution program*. Unpublished final report. Trident. Charleston, S.C.: United Way.

Hollinger, R.C., & Clark, J.P. (1983). Deterrence in the workplace: Perceived certainty, perceived severity, and employee theft. *Social Forces, 62,* 398–418.

Hudson, J., & Chesney, S. (1978). Research on restitution: A review and assessment. In B. Galaway and J. Hudson (Eds.) *Offender restitution in theory and action*. Toronto: Lexington.

Jacob, H. (1978). Rationality and criminality. *Social Science Quarterly, 59,* 584–585.

Jacob, H., & Lineberry, R.L. (1982). *Governmental responses to crime*. Washington, D.C.: U.S. Department of Justice, National Institute of Justice, June.

Jacob, H., & Rich, M.J. (1981). The effects of the police on crime: A second look. *Law and Society Review, 15,* 109–122.

Kahneman, D., Slovic, P., & Tversky, A. (1982). *Judgement under uncertainty: Heuristics and biases*. New York: Cambridge University Press.

Kahneman, D., & Tversky, A. (1972). Subjective probability: A judgement of representativeness. *Cognitive Psychology, 3,* 430–454.

Klein, M.W. (1987). Labeling theory and delinquency policy. *Criminal Justice and Behavior, 13.*

Kobrin, S. & Klein, M. (1982). *Community treatment of status offenders*. Beverly Hills: Sage.

Knorr, S. (1979). Deterrence and the death penalty: A temporal cross-sectional approach. *Journal of Criminal Law and Criminology, 70,* (2) 235–254.

Kraut, R.E. (1976) Deterrence and definitional influences on shoplifting. *Social Problems, 23,* 358–368.

Lanza-Kaduce, L. (1988). Perceptual deterrence and drinking and driving among college students. *Criminology, 26,* 321–343.

Lemert, E. (1967). *Human deviance, social problems and social control*. Englewood Cliffs, N.J.: Prentice-Hall.

Lempert, R. (1982). Organizing for deterrence: Lessons from a study of child support. *Law and Society Review, 16,* 513–568.

Lichtenstein, S., & Slovic, P. (1971). Reversals of preferences between bids and choices in gambling decisions. *Journal of Experimental Psychology, 89,* 46–55.

Lipton, D., Martinson, R., & Wilks, J. (1975). *The effectiveness of correctional treatment: A survey of treatment and evaluation studies*. New York: Praeger.

Lindbloom, C.E., & Braybrooke, D. (1963). *A strategy of decision*. New York: MacMillan.

Lloyd, M.R., & Joe, G.W. (1979). Recidivism comparisons across groups: Methods of estimation and tests of significance for recidivism rates and asymptotes. *Evaluation Quarterly, 3,* 105–117.

Logan, C. (1983). Problems in ratio correlation: The case of deterrence research. *Social Forces, 60,* March, 791–809.

Luckenbill, D. (1982). Compliance under threat of severe punishment. *Social Forces, 60,* March, 791–809.

Maltz, M., & McCleary, R. (1977). The mathematics of behavioral change: Recidivism and construct validity. *Evaluation Quarterly, 1,* 421–438.

Margolis, H. (1982). *Selfishness, altruism, and rationality: A theory of social choice*. Cambridge, Mass.: Cambridge University Press.

McCord, J. (1982). *A longitudinal appraisal of criminal sanctions*. Presented at the American Society of Criminology Annual meetings, Denver, Colo.

Meehl, P.E. (1977). The selfish voter paradox and the thrown away vote argument. *American Political Science Review,* 11–30.

Minor, W., & Harry, J. (1982). Deterrent and experiential effects in perceptual deterrence research: A replication and extension. *Journal of Research in Crime and Delinquency,* 190–203.

Moffitt, T. (1983). The learning theory model of punishment: Implications for delinquency research. *Criminal Justice and behavior, 10,* 131–158.

Murray, C., & Cox, L.A. (1979). *Beyond probation: Juvenile corrections and the chronic juvenile offender*. Beverly Hills: Sage.

Nagin, D. (1978). General deterrence: A review of the empirical evidence. In A. Blumstein, et al. (Eds.) *Deterrence and incapacitation: Estimating the effects of criminal sanctions on crime rates*. Washington, D.C.: National Academy of Sciences.

Nie, N., & Hull, C. (1983). *SPSSx*. Chicago, Ill: McGraw-Hill.

Orbell, J., Schwartz-Shea, P., & Simmons, R.T. (1984). Do cooperators exit more readily than defectors? *American Political Science Review, 78,* 147–162.

Paternoster, R.P., Saltzman, L., Chiricos, T.G., & Waldo, G.P. (1982). Perceived risk and deterrence: Methodological artifacts in perceptual deterrence research. *Journal of Criminal Law and Criminology, 73,* 1238–1257.

Paternoster, R.P., Saltzman, L.E., Waldo, G.P., & Chiricos, T.G. (1983). Estimating perceptual stability and deterrent effects. *Journal of Criminal Law and Criminology, 74,* 270–297.

Patterson, G.R. (1973). A social engineering technology for retraining the families of aggressive boys. In H.E. Adams & I.P. Unikel (Eds.), *Issues and trends in behavior therapy*. Springfield, Ill.: Thomas.

Phillips, L. & Votey, L., Jr. (1981). *The economics of crime control*. Beverly Hills: Sage.

Piliavin, I., Gartner, R., Thornton, C., & Matsueda, R. (1986). Crime deterrence, and choice. *American Sociological Review, 57,* 101–119.

Pogue, T.F. (1986). Offender expectations and identification of crime supply functions. *Evaluation Review, 10,* (4) Aug., 455–482.

Rapoport, A. (1985). Provision of public goods and the MCS experimental paradigm. *American Political Science Review, 79,* (1), Mar., 148–155.

Rawls, J. (1971). *A theory of justice*. Cambridge. Mass.: Harvard University Press.

Riker, W.H., & Ordeshook, P.C. (1968). A theory of the calculus of voting. *American Political Science Review, 61,* (1), March.

Ross, H.L., McCleary, R., & Epperlein, T. (1981–82). Deterrence of drinking and driving in France: An evaluation of the law of July 12, 1978. *Law and Society Review, 16,* (3) 365–373.

Ross, H.L. (1973). Law society and accidents: The British Road Safety Act of 1967. *Journal of Legal Studies, 2,* 1–78.

Rossi, P., et al. (1974). The seriousness of crimes: Normative structure and individual differences. *American Sociological Review, 39,* April, 224–237.

Sacco, V. (1984). an exploratory analysis of the conceptual meaning of perceptions of crime. *Canadian Journal of Criminology,* 295–306.

Saltzman, L., Paternoster, R., Waldo, G., & Chiricos, T.G. (1982). Deterrent and experiential effects: The problem of causal order in perceptual deterrence research. *Journal of Research in Crime and Delinquency,* July, 172–189.

Schneider, A. (1986). Restitution and recidivism rates of juvenile offenders: Results from four experimental studies. *Criminology, 24,* 533–552.

Schneider, A.L. (1982). The effects of deinstitutionalization of status offenders: A review essay. *Criminal Justice Abstracts,* 182–195.

Schneider, A.L., & Schneider, P.R. (1980). *The two-year report on the evaluation of the national juvenile restitution initiative.* Eugene, Ore.: Institute of Policy Analysis.

Schneider, A.L., & Schneider, P.R. (1984). A Comparison of programmatic and "ad hoc" restitution in juvenile courts. *Justice Quarterly,* 529–547.

Schneider, A.L., & Schneider, P.R. (1984). *The effectiveness of restitution as a sole sanction and as a condition of probation: Results from an experiment in Oklahoma County.* Stillwater, Okla.: Policy Sciences Group, Oklahoma State University.

Schneider, A.L., & Schneider, P.R. (1985). The impact of restitution on recidivism of juvenile offenders: An experiment in Clayton County, Georgia. *Criminal Justice Review, 10,* 1–10.

Schoemaker, P.J.H. (1980). *Experiments on decisions under risk: The expected utility hypothesis.* Boston: Martinus Nijhoff Publishing.

Schur, E.M. (1973). *Radical nonintervention: Rethinking the delinquency problem.* Englewood Cliffs, N.J.: Prentice-Hall.

Shapiro, P., & Votey, H.L., Jr. (1984). Deterrence and subjective probabilities of arrest: Modeling individual decisions to drink and drive in Sweden. *Law and Society Review, 18,* 583–601.

Sherman, L., & Berk, R.A. (1984). The specific deterrent effects of arrest for domestic assault. *American Sociological Review,* 261–271.

Shotland, R.L., & Mark, M.M. (Eds.) (1985). *Social science and social policy.* Beverly Hills: Sage.

Silberman, M. (1976). Toward a theory of criminal deterrence. *American Sociological Review, 41,* 442–461.

Simon, H. (1957). *Models of man: Social and rational.* New York: Wiley.

Simon, H. (1981). *The sciences of the artificial.* Cambridge, Mass.: M.I.T. Press.

Slovic, P. (1967). The relative influence of probabilities and payoffs upon perceived risk of gamble. *Psychonomic Science, 9,* 223–224.

Slovic, P., Fischoff, B., & Lichtenstein, S. (1977). Behavioral decision theory. *Annual Review of Psychology, 28,* 1–39.

Smith, C.F.W. (1981). *Rules and rates: The influence of anticipated and actual sanctions on longitudinal deviant outcomes.* Presented at the Annual Meeting of the American Society of Criminology, Washington, D.C.

Steinhurst, W. (1981). Hypothesis tests for limited failure survival distributions. *Evaluation Review, 5,* 699–711.

Stollmack, S., & Harris, C.J. (1974). Failure rate analysis applied to recidivism data. *Journal of Operations Research, 22,* 1192–1205.

Sutton, P. (1980). *Felony sentencing.* Washington, D.C.: National Institute of Justice.

Teevan, J.J., Jr. (1976). Subjective perception of deterrence (continued). *Journal of Research in Crime and Delinquency,* 155–163.

Thomas, C.W., & Bishop, D.M. (1985). The effect of formal and informal sanctions on delinquency: A longitudinal comparison of labeling and deterrence theories. *Journal of Criminal Law and Criminology, 75,* 1222–1245.

Tittle, C. (1969). Crime rates and legal sanctions. *Social Problems, 16,* 409–423.

Tittle, C. (1975). Deterrents or labeling? *Social Forces, 53,* 399–410.

Tittle, C. (1977). Sanction fear and the maintenance of social order. *Social Forces, 55,* 579–596.

Tittle, C.R. 1980). *Sanctions and social deviance: The question of deterrence.* New York: Praeger.

Tittle, C. (1985). Can social science answer questions about deterrence for policy use? In R. Shotland, et al. (Eds.), *Social science and social policy* (pp. 265–294). Beverly Hills: Sage.

Tversky, A., & Kahneman, D. (1974). Judgements under uncertainty: Heuristics and biases. *Science, 185,* Sept., 1124–1131.

Van De Kraft, A., Orbell, J.M., & Dawes, R.M. (1983). The minimal contributing set as a solution to public goods problems. *American Political Science Review, 77,* 112–122.

Waldo, G.P., & Chiricos, T.G. (1972). Perceived penal sanctions and self reported criminality: A neglected approach to deterrence research. *Social Problems, 19,* 522–540.

Watson, R. (1986). The effectiveness of increased police enforcement as a general deterrent. *Law and Society Review, 20,* 291–299.

Wax, M.L. (1977). *Effects of symbolic restitution and presence of victim on delinquent shoplifters.* Unpublished doctoral dissertation. Pullman, WA: Washington State University.

Wildavsky, A. (1987). Choosing preferences by construction institutions: A cultural theory of preference formation. *American Political Science Review, 81,* 3–21.

Williams, A.F., et al. (1975). The legal minimum drinking age and fatal motor vehicle crashes. *Journal of Legal Studies, 4,* 219–239.

Williams, K., & Hawkins, R. (1986). Perceptual research on general deterrence: A critical review. *Law and Society Review, 20,* 546–572.

Wilson, J.Q. (1983). *Crime and public policy.* San Francisco: Transaction Books.

Wilson, J.Q., & Boland, B. (1978). The effect of the police on crime. *Law and Society Review, 12,* 367.

Wilson, J.Q., & Herrnstein, R.J. (1985). *Crime and human nature.* New York: Simon and Schuster.

Wilson, M. (1983). *The juvenile offender instrument: Administration and a description of findings.* Eugene, Ore.: Institute of Policy Analysis.

Wolfgang, M.E., Figlio, R.M., & Sellin, T. (1972). *Delinquency in a birth cohert.* Chicago, Ill: University of Chicago Press.

Wright, G. (1984). *Behavioral decision theory.* Beverly Hills: Sage.

Zimring, F. (1978). Policy experiments in general deterrence: 1970–1975. In Blumstein, A., et al. (Eds.), *Deterrence and incapacitation: Estimating the effects of criminal sanctions on crime rates.* Washington, D.C.: National Academy of Sciences.

Zimring, F., & Hawkins, G. (1973). *Deterrence: The legal threat in crime control.* Chicago, Ill.: The University of Chicago Press.

Author Index

Subject Index

Research in Criminology

continued

Multiple Problem Youth:
Delinquency, Substance Use, and Mental Health Problems
D.S. Elliott, D. Huizinga and S. Menard

Selective Incapacitation and the Serious Offender:
A Longitudinal Study of Criminal Career Patterns
Rudy A. Haapanen

Deterrence and Juvenile Crime: Results from a National Policy Experiment
Anne L. Schneider

MIX
Papier aus verantwortungsvollen Quellen
Paper from responsible sources
FSC® C105338

If you have any concerns about our products,
you can contact us on
ProductSafety@springernature.com

In case Publisher is established outside the EU,
the EU authorized representative is:
Springer Nature Customer Service Center GmbH
Europaplatz 3, 69115 Heidelberg, Germany

Printed by Libri Plureos GmbH
in Hamburg, Germany